FOLK ART
QUILTS

ANNE HULBERT

HISTORICAL CONSULTANT **SHIELA BETTERTON**

MEREDITH® PRESS

To D.M.H. with V.M.T.

First published in Great Britain in 1992 by
Anaya Publishers Ltd, Strode House
44–50 Osnaburgh Street
London NW1 3ND

U.S. edition published by
Meredith® Press
150 East 52nd Street
New York, NY 10022
Meredith® Press is an imprint of Meredith® Books:
President, Book Group: Joseph J. Ward
Vice-President, Editorial Director: Elizabeth P. Rice

Copyright © Anaya Publishers Ltd 1992
Editor: Diana Brinton
Designer: Kathy Gummer
Photography: Tracey Orme
Illustrators: John Hutchinson
Anthony Duke
Mike Leaman

For Meredith® Press:
Executive Editor: Maryanne Bannon
Associate Editors: Guido Anderau,
Carolyn Mitchell, Ruth Weadock
Technical Consultant: Cheri Tamm Raymond

All correspondence should be
addressed to Meredith® Press

ISBN: 0–696–02396–2

Typeset by Bookworm Typesetting, Manchester
Colour reproduction by Scantrans Pte Ltd, Singapore
Printed and bound in Singapore by Times Offset Ltd

Distributed by Meredith Corporation, Des Moines, Iowa
This book may not be sold outside the United States of America.

CONTENTS

FOREWORD

The American Museum in Britain, which opened in 1961, is located in Claverton Manor, a late Georgian house designed by Sir Jeffry Wyatville around 1820. It is set within extensive grounds, commanding a fine view over the valley of the River Avon, yet is less than a ten-minute drive from the center of Bath. The Museum was founded by Dallas Pratt and John Judkyn, two men concerned with increasing Anglo-American understanding. Their aim was to interpret the history and decorative arts of the United States by showing, through furnished rooms and exhibitions, how Americans lived from colonial times to the end of the nineteenth century.

The main collection is arranged as a series of period rooms, many fitted with original panelling and floorboards brought from houses in the United States, and filled with fine examples of American craftsmanship. The rooms date from the late seventeenth century, the period of the first substantially built houses of the European settlers, until the time of the Civil War in the 1860s. These rooms not only show the achievements of American craftsmen, but present a living picture of domestic life, from the harsh practicalities of the early settlements, with their dependence upon Europe, to the increasing sophistication and refinement of the later eighteenth century and the ensuing development of a national style with regional characteristics.

The rooms and displays also show the diversity of cultures that give a distinctive flavor to the decorative arts of America: the Shakers, with their principles of order, harmony, and utility; the Pennsylvania Germans, with their love of highly decorated objects; the isolated Spanish colonists of New Mexico; the New England Puritans, and the North American Indians, whose various tribes were spread across the continent. Other exhibitions show the importance of ships for immigration, whaling or trade, and the pioneering spirit of the early Americans as they travelled westwards, seeking new territory or dreaming of gold. Throughout the museum are additional displays of American silver, pewter, and glass. One room is devoted to our important textile holdings, including hooked rugs, samplers, and the quilts that are the subject of this book.

Exhibitions continue in the grounds of the museum: a brightly painted Conestoga wagon from around 1830; a late nineteenth-century observation platform of a railroad car, which gave travellers a panoramic view of the surrounding countryside; an Indian tepee characteristic of the Plains, and a milliner's shop full of decorated bandboxes. As visitors explore the grounds they will come upon a handsome semi-circular building which originally housed the stables. This has been transformed into our Folk Art Gallery, containing a splendid collection of weathervanes, shop signs, portraits, cigar store figures, and paintings – all characterized by the vigorous forms and primitive designs inherent in the American folk art tradition. A short walk in the opposite direction will bring the visitor to the New Gallery. Completed in 1988, this modern building contains a temporary exhibition gallery, a map room with a splendid collection of printed maps from the fifteenth and sixteenth centuries, relating to the discovery of the New World, and a reference library specializing in American history and the decorative arts.

The gardens are one of the great features of the American Museum; there is a replica of George Washington's rose and flower garden from Mount Vernon – complete with a white picket fence and the schoolhouse where Washington is supposed to have taught his step-grandchildren. Other garden exhibitions include a colonial herb garden and a dye-plant border, showing the importance of specific plants and herbs for culinary, medicinal, aromatic and dyeing purposes. A major project recently carried out in the grounds was the transformation of an overgrown area into an arboretum devoted to a display of shrubs, ferns, and trees from the North American continent.

One of the best-known features of the American Museum remains the extensive collection of quilts. This book gives not only a sampling of our rich holdings in this popular folk art tradition, but practical instruction as well. The photographs allow the reader a glimpse into some of our period rooms. We are delighted to have Anne Hulbert as author of this book, and the museum's textile specialist, Shiela Betterton, as the historical consultant.

WILLIAM MCNAUGHT, Director

JUDITH ELSDON, Assistant Curator

PREFACE/HOW TO USE THIS BOOK

The art of quilt-making is enjoying ever-increasing popularity for, while materials may have changed, the basic, simple methods remain unaltered, and well within the reach of all. The quilts in this book are outstanding representatives of the folk art of their period – a truly eye-catching and inspiring selection with a fine range of pattern and color. It is a great privilege to have this opportunity of reproducing some of the treasures from the museum's large and magnificent collection.

Most quilts were made for practical purposes; they were well-used and given the loving care they deserved. They were also made for a lifetime and beyond, and repeated use and laundering over the years have taken their toll. Inevitably, therefore, some fading and shrinkage and distortion of the contours has occurred and, in a few areas, the quilting has almost disappeared. In one or two instances where the original quilting pattern is too difficult to make out, an alternative design has been suggested.

Not all the early quilt-makers were over-fastidious when measuring and cutting out their fabrics for piecing and applying; nor were they too concerned if shapes did not quite fit or exactly match one another. They would simply make a little tuck here or snip a bit there to put matters right. Notwithstanding this sometimes casual approach, their methods worked. The results are charming and the balance and symmetry in the designs of these masterpieces is surprisingly successful. However, the faithful reproduction of the inaccuracies is not really feasible in the space available and so, where necessary, I have altered the design marginally, to simplify the work.

The colors suggested are those used in the original quilts. While this is a help when it comes to identifying elements of the design, you can, of course, choose your own color variations to complement a particular scheme. Why not experiment also with fabrics; for example, by substituting prints for solids?

In the days when these quilts were made, the width of fabrics available usually depended upon the size of individual hand-made looms. Often, too, discarded garments and household articles were dismantled and re-used. It is hardly surprising, therefore, that there were so many seams in some of the backings and borders, and throughout the front of the 'Blue Calamanco' quilt. In contrast, I have aimed at minimizing the number of seams by recommending the most economical widths of fabric for the various quilts. Even so, you should study the instructions closely and carefully plan the cutting before you begin.

There is no reason why the sewing machine should not be used to join the blocks, sashings and borders together, and to bind the edges; machine stitching is strong and fast. The same applies to several areas of the pieced-work designs. Machine appliqué is another matter. You might consider this method of applying shapes, but remember how conspicuously it contrasts with the hand-sewn.

In this book, there is a quilt for everyone; from the complete beginner to the highly experienced needleworker. Even so, some of them, though simple enough, will require much time and patience. Certain quilts – 'Christmas Bride' or 'Ruth Porter's Quilt', for example – could nevertheless provide splendid and worthwhile enterprises for group quilt-making.

The book provides patterns and instructions for making quilts using appliqué and pieced work with several methods of quilting. Some are worked with a single technique, and others with a combination. At the end of the book are special sections on the techniques themselves, to help guide you through the various stages of reproducing these lovely works of art.

Why not create another generation of spectacular heirlooms!

ANNE HULBERT

7

INTRODUCTION

*I*T IS OFTEN ASSUMED that the first American quilts were made of patchwork, but although it has been ascertained from contemporary literature that quilting skills were taken to America by early colonists, there is no mention of patchwork. The Puritans considered needlework a virtuous occupation, and women emigrating from Europe took with them a knowledge of plain sewing, which probably included quilting. Textile skills were an important economic factor in the life of a woman in colonial days. It was essential for her to know how to prepare yarn and to make and repair all textile items in the home. Because early looms were so constructed that only geometric patterns could be woven, she also had to learn how to make decorative effects with her needle. Quilting was part of this work. Warm and comfortable beds were very necessary, and one of the housewife's main concerns was the making of bed furnishings. In the days when the best bed was often in the parlor, the exquisite stitchery on the bed furnishings was one way of showing a housewife's sewing and needlework skills.

The mother country did little to encourage textile manufacture in her American colonies, and despite the very early establishment of a textile factory at Rowley, Massachusetts, weaving remained largely a cottage industry until after the War of Independence. After 1630, many colonists brought sheep with them to America, so early textiles were of wool or linen, or a mixture of the two called linsey woolsey. Cotton did not become a staple crop until the 1760s.

Before the War of Independence, American best quilts were very similar to those made in Britain. Deprived of facilities to manufacture their own textiles, the American colonists had to import from Europe and the East by way of Britain. Second only to hardware. textiles from Bristol and London were the most necessary and popular imports. One Bristol firm alone employed 400 men to make serge for export to the American colonies. As the years passed, many other fabrics from Europe and the East became available, including calico, gingham, dimity, damask, huckaback and, by the end of the eighteenth century, copper-plate prints from France and England.

One of the most popular fabrics was calamanco, a fine worsted that was made in Norwich and exported to America, together with the sheep's wool for the padding. The British East India Company was founded in 1603, and by the 1630s Indian chintzes, calicoes and palampores (cotton bedspreads) were being brought to England and thence to the American colonies. They were considered far superior to those of European manufacture. When the palampores began to wear out, the best pieces were saved and applied to a new background, so making up a new piece of cloth. This technique was used to make some of the first appliqué bedcovers.

The British influence on American quilts is obvious from the use of the medallion format in the eighteenth and nineteenth centuries, before the repeated block technique became established. This method making one square of a given pattern at a time evolved gradually. It was well suited to the quick production of the bedcovers needed by every family. From it developed a host of patterns for, once several blocks of the same pattern had been made, there were any number of ways in which they could be put together to produce different designs. Before 1830, few quilt designs consisted solely of geometric shapes; it was more usual to have a pieced center with an appliqué border. The term 'patchwork' was so broadly used during the eighteenth century that today it is not always possible to know whether it refers to pieced work or appliqué.

As early as the first quarter of the eighteenth century, quilting had become a social accomplishment, particularly in urban areas, such as Boston, New York and Philadelphia, where it became an essential part of a young lady's education. At this time, both men and women worked as professional quilters in many of the major American cities.

The designs for American embroidery, and through embroidery for quilt patterns, came from many sources. Immigrants brought with them design traditions from their homelands, and patterns were also taken from imported books and herbals. Another source of design was the New World itself, which offered new types of flowers, trees and animals. At the beginning of the eighteenth century, dame schools and schools of embroidery were established, and teachers encouraged pupils to draw patterns. By the middle of the nineteenth century, one of the major forms of domestic folk art was the designing of quilt patterns.

Patterns for the pieced quilt tops were taken from a number of sources. Names such as Bear's Paw, Turkey Tracks, Churn Dash and Windmill tell their own story, as does the Rocky Road to California. Historical events also gave their name to patterns: Whig Rose reminds us of political events in the early days of the new United States, while Queen Charlotte's Crown is named after the last queen before the colonies broke free and became the United States of America. Other names were taken from the Bible and books such as *The Pilgrim's Progress*, which were widely read by the early settlers.

Many of the patterns are symbolic: oak leaves signify long life, pineapples stand for hospitality, and pomegranates for fruitfulness and immortality. The swastika is a very old symbol, known to both eastern and western peoples; shorn of its twentieth-century meaning, it is a mystic symbol of motion, but also means good fortune, health and a long life. Sometimes, a quilter would make a deliberate mistake in her work, following the old eastern belief that only Allah is perfect.

Lavishly appliquéd album quilts, of which this is a particularly fine example, were especially popular in the Baltimore area, and are hence referred to as 'Baltimore album quilts'. The geometric pieced hearts at the end of each sashing strip indicate that this was indeed made for a bride. One of the blocks is dated April 1st, 1847, and the quilt measures some 122in (310cm) square.

Until quite recently, most books written about colonial days in America have concentrated on the part played by men, but gradually journals and diaries written by women have been found. These were not written for the eyes of future generations, but as a chronicle of everyday happenings, and reading through them it is evident that textile skills and needlework were important well into the nineteenth century. Sometimes there is mention of patchwork, but more often the note reads 'put quilt in frame' or 'quilt finished, took out of frame'. One diarist writes of going to quilting and spinning 'frolics', and after one she confides 'I am almost wore up to the hub with so much spinning frolic.'

There are frequent references to little girls making patchwork while they learned the alphabet. Sometimes, sewing was used as a corrective measure, children being set to sewing patchwork until their behavior improved. A little girl was taught first to make a 4-patch, comprising four squares of fabric joined to make a larger square. This mastered, she then progressed to making a 9-patch, which consisted of nine squares, five of one fabric and four of another, joined alternately to make a greater square. As it was customary for a girl to have up to twelve quilts in her hope chest, perhaps even thirteen – the last and grandest one of all being her bride's quilt – she started piecing at an early age. One quilt in the museum's collection is marked on the reverse 'I. Sterrett, No.8'.

The continuing westward expansion, which lasted into the twentieth century, meant that there was always a need for warm bedding, and quilts were a necessity in days when homes were roughly built and poorly heated. Distances between homes were often great, and women had to cultivate interests that could be carried out in the home. Patchwork and quilting fulfilled this need. Cutting the pieces and putting them together could be a boring process, and it was very exacting. Without outside distractions, once everyday duties were finished, leisure meant time for sewing, and often the whole family joined in. Boys helped by cutting the patches; young girls took part in the sewing, and older girls assisted with the quilting. Families often lived far apart, and quilting bees – when women met to quilt together – provided welcome social occasions and were considered as important as church socials. Many quilting bees lasted a whole day, the women taking it in turns to sew. Those whose sewing was not up to standard threaded needles or served refreshments. When work was over for the day the men joined the party; quilt frames were put away, and supper was served, to be followed by games, music and often dancing.

The advent of the sewing machine in the 1850s proved a great boon to those who could afford one, and with the availability of fabrics printed with patchwork patterns, new clothes and household items could be made more quickly. Also, women began to piece their quilt tops by machine.

About the middle of the nineteenth century, a new style of patchwork emerged, called 'crazy' patchwork – crazy in the sense of cracked or crazed. The technique reached the height of its popularity during the last quarter of the century. Cotton patchwork came under the heading of plain sewing, but crazy patchork, made with silks, velvets, brocades and ribbons, and heavily embellished with embroidery, became socially acceptable. After the austerity of the Civil War, women felt they needed an outlet that would cheer up their homes and at the same time give them a satisfying hobby. The making of crazy patchwork, helped by the increased production of American silk, fulfilled this need.

One kind of quilt made in America but seldom in the British Isles was the album quilt. This was a co-operative effort, with each friend who wished to honor the recipient contributing a block. The blocks were usually signed and dated, and included motifs relevant to the recipient's life and interests.

The most elaborate and sophisticated album quilts are those made in Baltimore, Maryland, between 1843 and 1853. By the middle of the nineteenth century, Baltimore was a flourishing port and women could buy fabrics imported from Britain and France as well as those produced at home.

Another form of album quilt was the freedom quilt, made for a young man on reaching the age of 21. Sisters and girl friends pieced the top, which was then put away until the young man became engaged, when he would give it to his future bride to be added to those which she was making.

The United States of America is home to people of many nationalities, all of whom have left their mark on American culture and the American decorative arts. Quilts made by the Amish women, for example, are admired and copied. They are of simple geometric patterns, many being variations of the square rectangle and triangle. It was considered 'worldly' to have too many pieces in the quilt top, so the piecing is bold and in unusual color combinations.

Less well-known are those quilts made by slaves and African-American women; the Hawaiians have evolved their own style and techniques, and Sioux women of the Great Plains have also learned to make quilts – examples of all these types of quilt can be found in the museum's collection.

This then is the background to the quilts in the collection of the American Museum in Britain. Some years before the museum opened in 1961, the co-founders, Dallas Pratt and John Judkyn were collecting American quilted bedcovers. In May 1958, Mr Judkyn staged an exhibition of his collection of British quilts, together with some loaned by the Shelburne Museum in Vermont, at his house near Bath. This was possibly the first time that American quilts were publicly exhibited in Britain, long before the great quilt revival of the 1970s, and the occasion marked the beginning of the quilt collection at the American Museum. This is considered the best outside the United States and ranks high among collections there. Thanks to the generosity of many people on both sides of the Atlantic, there are now about 170 quilts in the collection, of which 50 are displayed at all times in the museum's textile room.

SHIELA BETTERTON
Textile and Needlework Specialist

APPLIQUE QUILTS

*I*N MEDIEVAL TIMES, when fabrics were scarce and expensive, the best pieces were cut from worn-out textiles and sewn to a background fabric to make a new piece of cloth. This was the technique used in later years for some of the first appliqué bedcovers. Appliqué patterns can take the form of a single large design, resembling a painting, or of a smaller motif, made into blocks which are then joined together in the same way as pieced work. Designs, particularly those of leaves and flowers, were often drawn freehand.

Abstract patterns could be made by the simple folded paper cut-out technique, used to great effect on Hawaiian quilts.

Covers were generally, though not always, quilted, not only for warmth, but for the three-dimensional effect that this gave to the shapes. Sometimes, this effect was further enhanced by inserting an additional padding of fine cotton behind certain shapes.

There is little evidence to support the belief that appliqué quilts were kept for best and pieced quilts were for everyday use.

OAK LEAVES

Nineteenth-century quilts often featured red and green shapes on a white background. White cotton was cheap, and the introduction into America in about 1830 of the 'Turkey Red', long known in the East, meant that for the first time, there was a permanent red dye. The strong, slightly austere design of this handsome quilt, with its 'hint of Christmas' coloring, is considerably relieved by the softness of a lovely swirling border.

The maker of the original must have been in a quandary over her corners, as each is completely different and hence tiresome to reproduce exactly. Consequently, the corners have been made symmetrical. Also, two of the side lattice strips need to be fractionally narrower than the rest in order to accommodate the border appliqué. These minor adjustments in no way affect the appeal of this fine quilt. A narrow green binding, matching the leaves, edges the quilt.

SIZE

Approximately 92in × 74in (233cm × 187cm)

MATERIALS REQUIRED
All fabrics 36in (90cm) wide
For the quilt top and border:
8½yds (7.75m) of white cotton
For the backing: 9yds (8.25m) of white cotton
For the appliqué: 2¾yds (2.5m) of plain red cotton
For appliqué and binding:
2 ⅛yds (1.95m) of plain green cotton
9yds (8.25m) of thin lightweight batting
Matching white, red and green threads

Cut out the quilt top
All pieces are cut on the straight grain of the fabric.
Note: ¼in (6mm) seams *are* allowed for.
From the white cotton, cut the pieces listed below.

12 blocks (A), each 13½in (34cm) square

Lattice sashing strips, 4½in (11.5cm) wide: nine horizontal (B), 13½in (34cm) long; two vertical (C), 64½in (163cm) long; two strips (D), 47½in (120cm) long, for the ends

Two narrow strips (E), 4in (10cm) wide and 72½in (183.5cm) long, are required for the sides

Bordered with a particularly charming ribbon and leaf design, the nineteenth-century quilt from Lancaster County, Pennsylvania, seen on the preceding pages, features oak leaves, a symbol of long life.

The border strips, all 10¼in (26cm) wide: two for the ends of the quilt (F), 54½in (137.5cm) long; and two for the sides (G), 92in (234cm) long

Mark and cut the appliqué shapes
1 Trace all the template patterns required (see overleaf and page 105) and mark each one with its appropriate identification. Prepare and cut templates (see pages 96 and 102).
Note: seams are *not* included on appliqué templates.
2 Mark shapes so that when they are applied their grainlines will run with those of the background fabric. Lay the templates on the fabric and mark around them; leaving at least ½in (12mm) between shapes, for seam allowances.

On the red cotton mark 12 flower centers (H), 48 flower petals (I), and 32 ribbons (J).

On the green cotton mark 48 large leaves (K), 28 border leaves (L), and 28 small border leaves (M).

3 Also on the green cotton, mark strips (N), 1in (2.5cm) wide, on the straight grain of the fabric, for binding the edge of the quilt. A total length of 9½yds (8.75m) will be required, so several seams will be necessary. Avoid joining strips in such a way that the seams will fall at the corners of the quilt, as they will not easily lie flat, and they will also look untidy.
4 From the red and green fabrics cut all the pieces (H–M), making them ¼in (6mm) larger all around than the marked shape, to allow for seams.
5 Staystitch around the edges of the appliqué shapes, and clip curves and notches (see page 96). Turn under and baste all the edges, except those that will be overlapped.
6 Cut and join the green binding strips, N (seam allowances *are* included in the width measurement).

Work the appliqué
As the oak leaves practically fill the blocks, care must be taken to ensure that ample seam allowances are left at the sides; the tops of the leaves must not be caught in the seams. Each block is made in the same way.
1 Mark or baste diagonal guidelines, one each way, from corner to corner across the block. This will help in positioning the appliqué, and will also mark the center of the design.
2 Pin the appliqué shapes in position as follows: first the flower center (H); then the oak leaves (K), so that the raw edges of leaves and centre points abut together; lastly, pin the petals (I), so that the turned-under seam covers the raw edges of the leaf and petal.
3 Baste and then stitch the prepared shapes, using

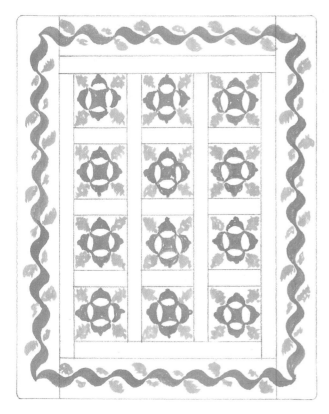

matching threads. Lap areas over or under one another as necessary, where shown on the templates.

4 Finish the appliqué as explained on page 97.

5 Stitch the remaining eleven blocks to match.

Piece the top

Note: ¼in (6mm) seam allowances *are* included.

1 With right sides facing; join the blocks: stitch the nine short horizontal sashing strips (B) to the twelve blocks (A) to make three vertical rows of four blocks each.

2 Join the rows of blocks together, alternating with the two vertical strips (C).

3 Join on the two horizontal strips (D) across the width at each end, then add the vertical strips (E) to each side.

4 With right sides facing, stitch the two shorter border strips (F) across each end, then stitch the two longer border strips (G) to each side.

Work the border appliqué

Using the recommended methods, prepare, stitch and finish the appliqué. Note that the border oak leaves alternate their positions, but they are not reversed; care

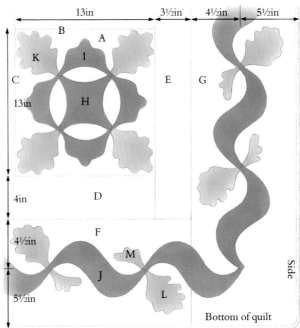

*The border quilting pattern indicated
is given on page 105.*

4 Stitch the appliqué borders at the other end, and on both side strips (G) in the same manner, in each case starting at the center.

Quilting and finishing

1 From the pattern given, mark the completed quilt face with lines for outline quilting on the oak leaves, the flowers and the ribbons, as shown on the templates. Also mark the design for the trailing flower and leaf border quilting (on page 105).

2 Cut out and join the batting and backing so that each measures 92in × 74in (233cm × 187cm).

3 Baste the quilt face, batting and backing firmly together.

4 Quilt all marked lines. The threads used for quilting should match the background fabric of the top face of the quilt.

5 Round off all the corners slightly for easier binding, and trim all around the edges of the three layers of the quilt to make them straight and level. Baste the layers firmly together near the edge, all around.

6 Bind the edges of the quilt with the narrow green strips: with right sides facing, baste and stitch the binding all around to the front face of the quilt, easing it around the corners; fold the binding over to the back; turn under the ¼in (6mm) allowance, and neatly hem down, making sure the stitching is not visible on the front.

7 Press lightly.

is needed to place them correctly. Wherever necessary, lap raw edges under adjacent shapes, to avoid creating too much bulk.

1 Start at the center of one end strip (F) and pin the prepared ribbon pieces along the border towards the corners, spacing them to 9in (23cm) centers. The seams (X) where the ends of the ribbons meet should be 4½in (11.5cm) from the seamline with the sashing strips (E and D).

2 Tuck the raw ends of the stems of the prepared border leaves (L and M) underneath the ribbon seams (X) and pin them into place.

3 When the appliqué is satisfactorily positioned, baste and stitch all shapes down.

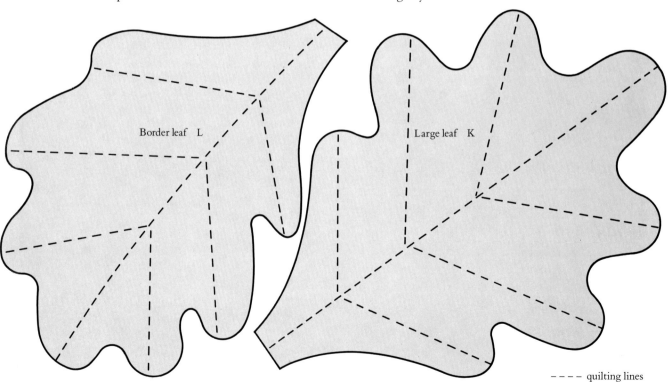

Border leaf L

Large leaf K

– – – – quilting lines

18

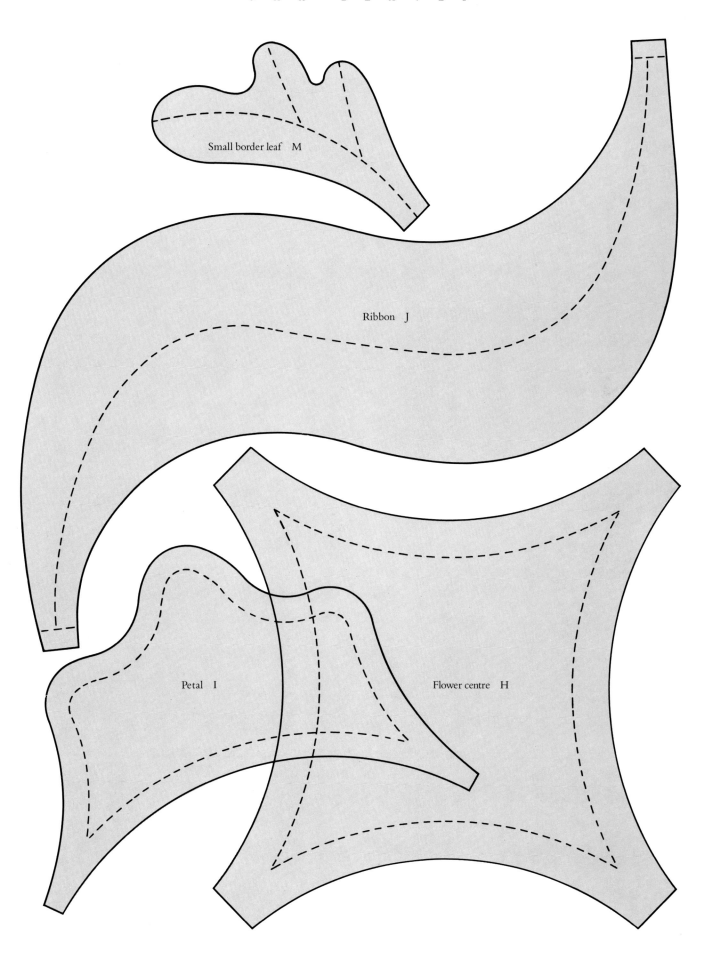

Small border leaf   M

Ribbon   J

Petal   I

Flower centre   H

PINEAPPLES

The pineapple, a native of South America, often symbolizes hospitality. It was widely used both as an appliqué pattern and in quilting, as well as to decorate objects as diverse as teapots and gateposts. Cotton seeds remain in the padding of this quilt.

The arrangement of these superb pineapples – six facing one way and six the other – creates a perfect balance in this bold, and beautifully designed quilt. As well as edging the quilt, the elegant border of bows and swags softens the strength of the repetitive design.

The bows on the long sides of the border are arranged slightly closer together than the bows along the short ends, and the swags on the long sides are tucked slightly further under the bows. These alterations make it possible to regularize the border design while adhering almost to the original. They will be barely noticeable on the finished quilt.

SIZE
Approximately 99in × 80.5in (251cm × 205.5cm)

MATERIALS REQUIRED
All fabrics 36in (90cm) wide
For the quilt top and border: 7yds (6.4m) of white or cream cotton
For the backing: 8½yds (7.6m) of white or cream cotton
For the appliqué: 2½yds (2.3m) of plain cotton
For appliqué, sashing strips and binding: 3½yds (3.2m) of plain orange cotton
8½yds (7.6m) of thin lightweight batting
Matching threads

Cut out the quilt top

All pieces should be cut on the straight grain of the fabric.
Note: ¼in (6mm) seams *are* allowed for.
From the white cotton cut the pieces listed below.
12 blocks (A), each 17½in (44.5cm) square
Border bands, all 11in (28cm) wide: two (B) 59½in (152cm) long, for the ends, and two (C) 99½in (253cm) long, for the sides

The regularity of the bows and swags applied to the border of the border of this magnificent quilt combines well with the uniformity and boldness of the pineapple design. The quilt was made about 1850 by Leila Adams Weston and was the gift of the late Mrs Dorothy Weston.

Mark and cut the appliqué shapes

1 Trace all the template patterns required for appliqué and mark each with its appropriate indentifications. Prepare and cut out templates (see page 96).
Note: seam allowances are *not* included on the templates and, when marking, try to ensure that the straight grain of the shape is in alignment with that of the base fabric.
2 Mark around the templates onto the fabric, leaving at least ½in (12mm) between shapes, for seam allowances.

On green cotton, mark 12 large leaves (D), 12 tufts (E), 12 stems (F), 24 small leaves (G) – 12 of which should be reversed (flopped), and 28 swags (H).

On the orange cotton, mark 12 pineapples (I), 56 bow pieces (J) – 28 of which should be reversed, 28 knot pieces (K), and 56 bow tail pieces (L) – 28 of which should be reversed.

3 Cut out all marked shapes (D–L), cutting ¼in (6mm) out from the marked lines, to allow for seams. Keep shapes in labelled plastic bags until required.
4 Turning and basting the edges (see page 97), prepare enough appliqué shapes to complete one block.

Mark and cut out the sashing strips and binding strips

On the orange cotton, mark the latice sashing strips and quilt binding strips–¼in (6mm) seams *are* allowed for. Mark all sashing and binding strips 2½in (6.5cm) wide.
1 For the lattice, mark as follows: 9 horizontal (M), 17½in (44.5cm) long; 2 vertical (N), 74½in (190cm) long; 2 horizontal (O), 55½in (141.5cm) long, and 2 vertical (P), 78½in (200.5cm) long.
2 Also on the orange cotton, mark the border strips 2½in (6.5cm) wide: 2 horizontal (Q), 81in (207cm) long, for the ends, and 2 vertical (R), 99½in (254cm) long, for the sides.
3 Cut out all strips.

Work the appliqué

Always use threads to match the appliqué shapes.
1 Mark or baste diagonal guidelines, one each way, across one block (A) to assist the positioning of the appliqué.
2 Apply the prepared shapes in the following order, using the diagram for reference: pin the stem (F) into the corner; pin the large leaves (D), the pineapple (I) and the tuft (E), and then pin the small leaves (G) in place. Tuck any raw edges underneath adjacent shapes at this stage, as marked on the templates.
3 Using matching threads, baste and stitch the appliqué as pinned. Lap shapes over or under one another, as marked on the template patterns.

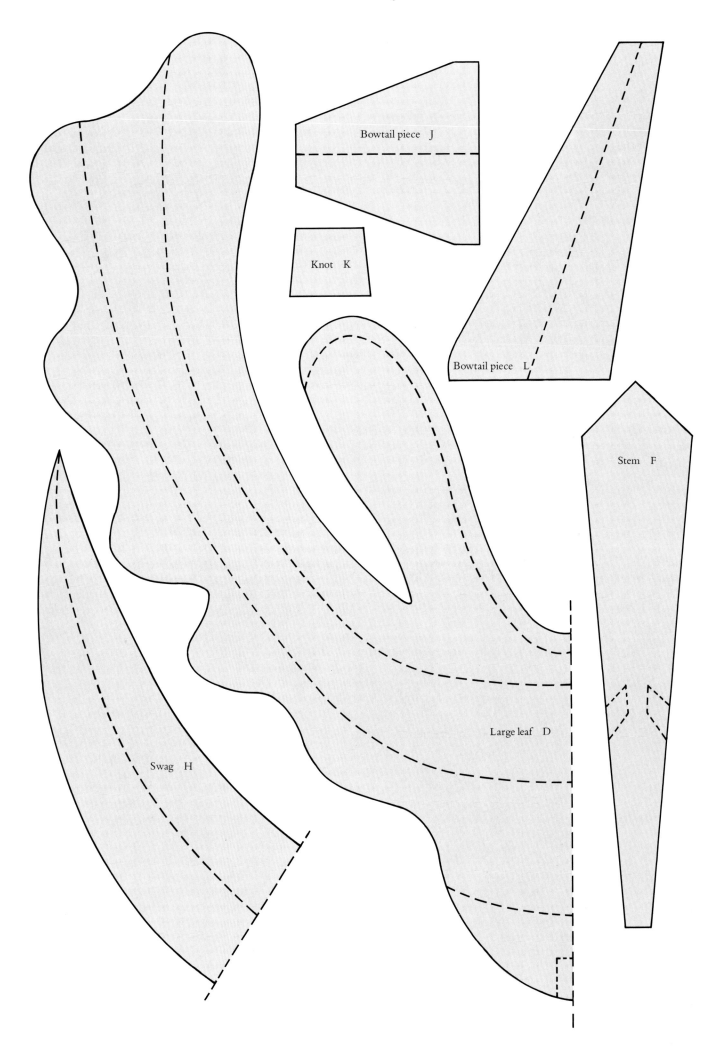

Bowtail piece   J

Knot   K

Bowtail piece   L

Stem   F

Large leaf   D

Swag   H

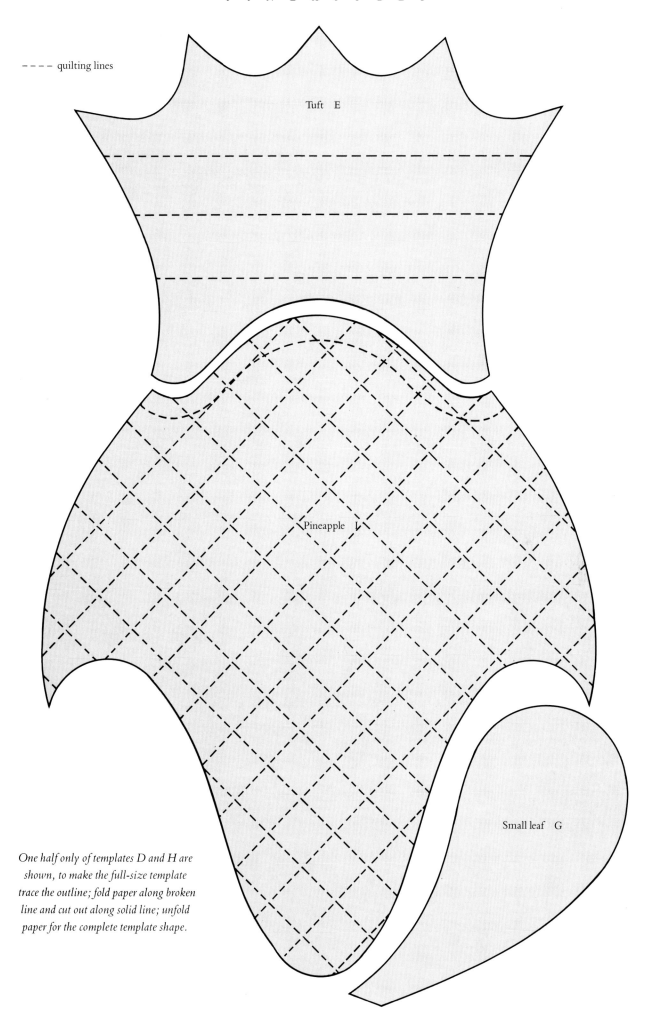

- - - - quilting lines

Tuft   E

Pineapple   D

Small leaf   G

One half only of templates D and H are shown, to make the full-size template trace the outline; fold paper along broken line and cut out along solid line; unfold paper for the complete template shape.

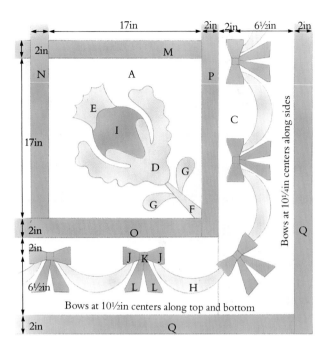

Bows at 10¼in centers along sides

Bows at 10½in centers along top and bottom

4 Finish the appliqué as explained on pages 97–98.

5 Make the remaining 11 blocks in the same manner.

Piece the top

Arrange the blocks as shown in the assembly diagram – six facing one way and six facing the other.

1 Stitch the nine short orange horizontal sashing strips (M) to 12 blocks (A), making three vertical rows of four blocks.

2 Join the rows of blocks together with the two vertical strips (N) running the length of the vertical rows.

3 Join on the two horizontal strips (O) across the width at each end.

4 Add the vertical strips (P) to each side.

5 Stitch the two shorter border strips (B) to the quilt, stitching across the width at each end.

6 Add the longer strips (C) to each side.

Work the border appliqué

Prepare, stitch and finish the swags and bows for the appliqué. Care must be taken to create as uniformly spaced a design as possible; it is therefore better to start at the center of each border and work towards the corners, into which any slight discrepancies may be eased.

Note that, in order to fit the dimensions of the quilt precisely, the bow spacing along the sides needs to be slightly less than that along the ends, as indicated. Thus, the swag ends along the sides should be tucked slightly further under the bows.

1 Pin the bows and knots in place along each end of the quilt with all the centers of the knots 2in (5cm) from the outer edge of the orange sashing and spaced 10½in (26.5cm) apart.

2 Pin the bows and knots in place along the sides, also with their centers 2in (5cm) from the edge of the sashing, but spaced only 10¼in (26cm) apart.

3 Baste and stitch the border appliqué all around the quilt.

Prepare for quilting

1 On the right side of the quilt top, mark the stitching lines for outline quilting on the pineapple tufts, leaves, swags and bows. Also mark lines, diagonally each way across the quilt face and spaced ¾in (2cm) apart, to make the all-over diamond pattern.

2 Cut and join batting to make an area measuring 99in x 80.5in (251cm × 205.5cm), and repeat with the backing fabric. Baste the completed quilt face, batting and backing together.

3 Trim around all edges of the three layers of the quilt and baste them together around the edges.

4 With right sides facing, baste and stitch one of the shorter binding strips (Q) across one end of the backing of the assembled quilt. Fold the strip over to the front to form a 2¼in (5.7cm) border on the front. Turn under ¼in (6mm); baste and, using blind stitch, neatly hem down. Repeat with the binding strip at the other end.

5 Baste under ¼in (6mm) across each end of one of the remaining orange strips (R). With right sides facing, baste and stitch this strip to one side of the quilt and fold it over to the front. Turn under ¼in (6mm), baste, and neatly hem down with blind stitch. Neatly slipstitch across the folds at each end. Repeat for the binding strip along the other side.

6 Mark pairs of diagonal lines, ¼in (6mm) apart, the pairs being set every ¾in (2cm) apart, all around the orange binding strips.

Quilt

Use green and orange threads to match the appliqué fabrics. For the background quilting, use matching cream or white threads.

The quilting is worked only up to the appliqué shapes, not across them.

1 Follow the broken quilting lines given on the template patterns for the pineapples, tufts, leaves, bows and swags. The stalks and small leaves are not quilted.

2 The entire background and lattice sashing of the quilt face is quilted in an all-over diamond pattern, and the edges are quilted in pairs of diagonals as marked.

BASEBALLS

This unpadded coverlet, in which the simplicity of the repeated baseball design is relieved by chain stitch embroidery, may have been made by several people. The Hall of Fame and National Museum of Baseball at Cooperstown, New York, credits Abner Doubleday with inventing baseball in 1839; the first organized game was played in 1845, and the first professional team (1869) was the Cincinnati Red Stockings.

The designer of the original limited her colors to navy blue and red for the appliqué baseballs, but the use of a greater variety of eye-catching colored prints might produce an even prettier, and possibly more interesting quilt. Solid circles appliquéd on a printed background, with a printed backing, might well be considered. This is a simple design to reproduce. The appliqué was worked on unbleached muslin, and the same fabric was used for the backing.

Although the quilting is limited, it is effective for this style of quilt – just a line of running stitches around the inside of the seams of every block. Chain stitch is embroided in white around all the circles, and diagonally across the intersections of the blocks. In the middle of the quilt there are six hearts worked in chain stitch.

The edges are finished in a neat and easy way, by bringing the backing over to the front.

SIZE
Approximately 77in × 66in (195.5cm × 167.5cm)

MATERIALS
All fabrics 36in (90cm) wide
For the quilt top: 5¾yds (5.3m) of pre-shrunk, unbleached or cream cotton
For the backing: 6½yds (5.9m) of pre-shrunk unbleached muslin
For the appliqué: ¾yd (70cm) of red printed cotton and the same of blue printed cotton
Cream cotton or rayon yarn for the chain stitch embroidery
Matching sewing threads

Make the templates and prepare shapes
Note: ¼in (6mm) seams are allowed for.
1 Make a 6in (15cm) square template and, cutting on the straight grain of the fabric, mark and cut 168 plain cotton blocks (A), for the quilt face.
2 Draw and cut out a circle (B), 3in (7.5cm) in diameter, in cardboard or plastic, for the baseball template.
3 Mark around template (B) on the red cotton print 84 times; then on the blue cotton print, also 84 times. Cut out all shapes.
4 Staystitch and clip all around the edge of each circle,

A
5½in square

B
2½in diameter

chain stitching

– – – quilting lines

Each circle is surrounded by a line of chain stitching, and chain-stitched lines also radiate out towards each corner.

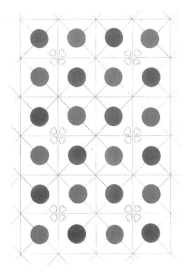

The key plan shows the center of the quilt only, with its six clusters of hearts, not found elsewhere on the quilt.

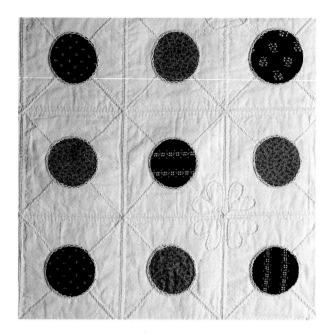

then turn under and baste around the edges.

Work the appliqué

1 Position a prepared circle (B) centrally on one of the blocks (A) and baste down.

2 Stitch all around and remove basting threads.

3 Cut away the backing fabric behind the applied shapes, and finish off the appliqué as instructed on pages 97–98.

4 Apply each baseball to a block in the same manner.

Join the blocks and assemble the top

The blocks may be joined by machine. Note that they are arranged to make alternate rows of red and blue baseballs in each direction.

1 With right sides facing, first baste and stitch the blocks together to make 12 strips, each with 14 blocks.

2 Join the strips together to complete the top, making sure that you align the seams and corners carefully.

3 Trim away ¼in (6mm) all around the finished top.

Quilting and finishing

1 On the front of the top, mark the stitching lines for the six clusters of hearts, placing them at alternate intersections of the blocks at the center of the quilt, as indicated in the drawing.

2 Cut out and join strips of backing; before trimming the edges straight, check that the backing measures ¾in (2cm) larger all around than the quilt top, to allow for the turnover to the front. Baste the completed quilt top and the backing together.

Trace the heart shapes (above right) and make a template to mark the stitching lines for the chain-stitched hearts.

3 Work a small running stitch along each side of all the seams that join the blocks together.

4 Embroider chain stitch around the edge of the baseballs.

5 Mark and embroider chain stitch hearts, 1½in (4cm) high, in the corners of the intersections of the 24 central blocks – six blocks long and four blocks wide, as shown in the drawing. You should end up with six clusters of four hearts each in the center of the quilt.

6 Now chainstitch diagonally across each block between the appliqué shapes, except in the immediate vicinity of the embroidered clusters of hearts.

7 The edges are self-bound, by bringing the backing over to the front, to make a ½in (12mm) binding when finished. Fold under the ¼in (6mm) seam allowance all around the single layer of the edges of the backing and press. Bring the backing over to the front, easing it around the corners; baste and hem down.

8 Lightly press the bound edges.

Six quilted hearts around the center of this simple coverlet, photographed on a dresser in Conkey's Tavern, and made in the nineteenth century in Cooperstown, New York State, would indicate that this quilt might have been made for a marriage.

TULIPS AND RIBBONS

The tulip, which reached Europe from Turkey in the mid-sixteenth century, and has been a popular motif in Western art ever since, is often used for both appliqué and quilting patterns.

The women of Pennsylvania, descendants of settlers from the Rhineland and Switzerland, loved the bright colors of the aniline dyes that were discovered in the mid-nineteenth century. In their quilts, they generally restricted themselves to only three colors, used to striking effect.

Although it may not appear so, at first glance, this lively and colorful cover is one for the absolute beginner. The appliqué is simplicity itself: large and uncomplicated shapes, with easy-to-stitch outlines, and a clear design to arrange. Lattice sashing has not been used, and the coverlet is not padded. The framework of the contrasting geometric border of pieced triangles provides the strong definition that the appliqué 'picture' well deserves.

As with several examples in this book, the corners of the maker's border have had to be adjusted to provide a uniform pattern and dependable and straightforward templates. The popular self-bound method of finishing the edge is used here, the edge of the backing being brought over to the front and sewn down, to make a narrow binding.

SIZE
Approximately 100¾in × 84½in (256cm × 215cm)

MATERIALS
All fabrics 36in (90cm) wide
For the quilt top, pieced zigzag and borders: 7¾yds
(7.1m) of white cotton
For the backing: 7½yds (7m) of white cotton
For appliqué: 2yds (1.8m) of green printed cotton;
2yds (1.8m) of plain yellow cotton,
and 1yd (90cm) of red printed cotton
For the zigzag border: 1yd (90cm) of deep red
printed cotton
Matching threads

Cut out the quilt top
All pieces are cut on the straight grain of the fabric.
Note: ¼in (6mm) seams *are* allowed for.
From the white cotton cut the pieces listed below.
   20 blocks (A), each 16¾in (42.5cm) square
· 2 border strips (B), each 6¾in (17cm) wide and 72in
(183cm) long, for the ends
   2 border strips (C), each 6¾in (17cm) wide and
100¾in (256cm) long, for the sides

Make the appliqué templates
Trace all the appliqué templates required and mark each one appropriately. Prepare and cut templates (see page 96).

Mark and cut the appliqué shapes
Note: seams are *not* allowed for on appliqué shapes.
1 The straight grain of the shapes to be applied should lie in the same direction as that of the ground fabric.
Lay the templates on the fabric and mark around them, leaving at least ½in (12mm) between each, for turning allowances.
   On the green cotton mark 40 stems (D), and 160 ribbons (E).
   On the yellow cotton mark 80 tulip petals (F), and 80 petals (F) reversed (flopped).
   On the red cotton mark 80 tulip centres (G).
2 From the red, green and yellow fabrics, cut out all the pieces required, making them ¼in (6mm) larger all around, to allow for turnings.
3 Staystitch round the edges and clip curves and corners (see page 97), turn under and baste the edges that are not to be under-lapped.

Mark the zigzag border triangles
The short sides of the triangles are right angles and should lie on the straight grain of the fabric.
1 On the deep red cotton mark 176 large triangles (H), and 20 small (I). Mark the wrong side of the fabric.
2 On the remainder of the white cotton from the quilt face mark 176 large triangles (H), and 28 small (I).
3 Cut out all the large (H) and small (I) triangles, making them ¼in (6mm) larger all around, to allow for turnings. Put them aside until required.

Work the appliqué
The tulips come quite near the edge of the block; take care not to catch them in the seams.
1 Mark or baste diagonal guidelines, from corner to corner, on a block. This will assist the positioning of the appliqué, and will determine the centre point.
2 Pin the appliqué shapes in position as follows: leaving raw edges at the ends, pin the stems (D) to form a cross

The tulip, which was accepted in Germany as a variation of the Holy Lily, the flower symbolizing the Trinity, was frequently used as a motif on Pennsylvania-German quilts. This typical example was made some time about 1860.

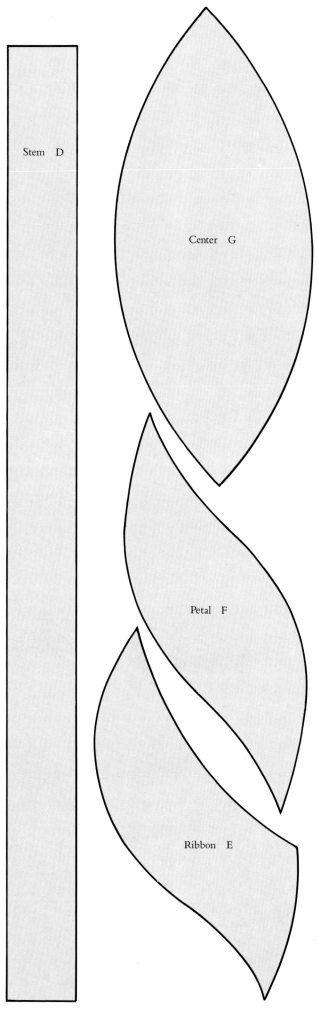

Stem D

Center G

Petal F

Ribbon E

in the center, pin the red centers (G) over the raw ends of the stems; pin on the yellow petals (F), with the raw edges at the sides tucked underneath the side edges of the center: complete the tulips, and lastly pin on the ribbons.

3 Baste and stitch the prepared shapes, using matching threads and tucking raw edges under adjacent shapes where necessary. Finish off the appliqué as explained on pages 97–98.

4 Following the same order, work the remaining 19 blocks to match.

Join the blocks

Note: ¼in (6mm) seams *are* allowed for.

With right sides facing, stitch the blocks together to make four rows of five blocks, then stitch the rows together to complete the quilt center.

Make the zigzag border

Each section of the four zigzag border edges is made from two long strips; these are joined together lengthways, and at the same time the triangles are staggered to form a zigzag pattern. Start by making the borders for the top and bottom edges.

1 Beginning and ending with one small white triangle (I), join large white and red triangles (H) alternately together to make a zigzag strip 65½in (166.5cm) long.

2 Beginning and ending with one small red triangle, make a second strip of alternately joined large red and white triangles, also 65½in (166.5cm) long.

3 Stitch the two pieced rows together lengthwise so that the triangles are staggered to create a zigzag effect in the deep red print.

4 With right sides facing, stitch the pieced border to top end of the quilt.

Repeat steps 1–4 for the zigzag border at the bottom end.

5 Now make the side borders. The side zigzag is

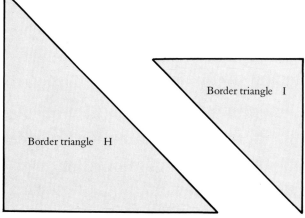

Border triangle H

Border triangle I

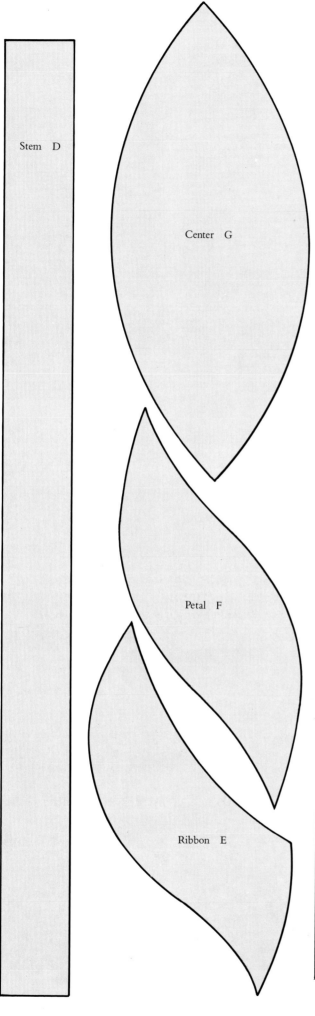

in the center, pin the red centers (G) over the raw ends of the stems; pin on the yellow petals (F), with the raw edges at the sides tucked underneath the side edges of the center: complete the tulips, and lastly pin on the ribbons.

3 Baste and stitch the prepared shapes, using matching threads and tucking raw edges under adjacent shapes where necessary. Finish off the appliqué as explained on pages 97–98.

4 Following the same order, work the remaining 19 blocks to match.

Join the blocks

Note: ¼in (6mm) seams *are* allowed for.

With right sides facing, stitch the blocks together to make four rows of five blocks, then stitch the rows together to complete the quilt center.

Make the zigzag border

Each section of the four zigzag border edges is made from two long strips; these are joined together lengthways, and at the same time the triangles are staggered to form a zigzag pattern. Start by making the borders for the top and bottom edges.

1 Beginning and ending with one small white triangle (I), join large white and red triangles (H) alternately together to make a zigzag strip 65½in (166.5cm) long.

2 Beginning and ending with one small red triangle, make a second strip of alternately joined large red and white triangles, also 65½in (166.5cm) long.

3 Stitch the two pieced rows together lengthwise so that the triangles are staggered to create a zigzag effect in the deep red print.

4 With right sides facing, stitch the pieced border to top end of the quilt.

Repeat steps 1–4 for the zigzag border at the bottom end.

5 Now make the side borders. The side zigzag is

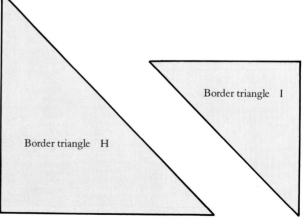

finished with four pieced squares at each end to make neat corners. Beginning and ending with a small red triangle (I), join large red and white triangles (H) alternately together to make a strip of pieced zigzag, 81¾in (207.5cm) long.

6 Make two squares, each using one small red and one small white triangle (I). Join one square to each end of the pieced strip, matching the red triangles to continue the zigzag.

7 Beginning and ending with a small white triangle (I), make a second strip of alternately joined large white and red triangles, also 81¾in (207.5cm) long.

8 Make two more squares, each using two small white triangles (I), and join one to each end of the two pieced zigzag strips.

9 Join the strips lengthwise, staggering the triangles to create the zigzag effect.

10 With right sides facing, stitch the pieced border to one side of the quilt.

Repeat steps 5–10 to make the zigzag border for the other side of the quilt.

Finish the outer border

With right sides facing, stitch the two shorter border strips (B) across each end of the quilt, then with right sides facing, stitch the two longer border strips (C) to each side.

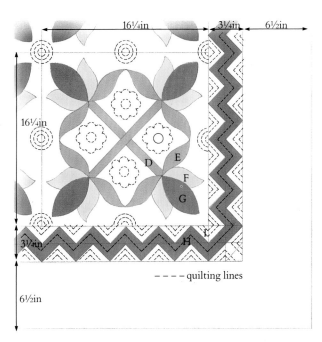

The rose-shaped quilting pattern that is placed at the angle of the crossed stems is given on page 107.

Quilting and finishing

1 On the top of the quilt, mark a rose in each of the angles of the crossed stems. Mark triple circles over the intersections of the blocks, and on the seams (see pages 106–107) mid-way between the intersections.

There is no need to mark the quilting lines on the pieced zigzag border, as the stitching can easily be done by eye from the patterns given.

2 Cut out and join the backing to make an area measuring ½in (12mm) larger all around than the quilt top, to allow for turning the backing to the front.

3 Baste the completed quilt top and the backing together (see page 108).

4 Quilt all marked lines, using thread that matches the background fabric of the top of the quilt.

The quilting on the pieced border simply consists of a single line of stitching following the up-and-down run of the red zigzag design.

On the white triangles, two lines are quilted parallel to the right angles.

5 Baste the edges together all around the quilt, leaving the ½in (12mm) seam extension free. Bring the backing over to the front. Fold under ¼in (6mm) all round and hem down.

CHRISTMAS BRIDE

The appliqué hearts and holly leaves were originally cut from green fabric, but the green used at that time was an unstable dye, which has faded and washed out. As it was considered unlucky to put hearts on anything other than a bride's quilt, perhaps this quilt was made for a girl marrying at Christmas time. Certainly, with its abundance of mistletoe hearts and holly wreaths, it must be one of the most romantic quilts of all, and would make the perfect present for a Christmas wedding.

While the green leaves have faded, the bright red berries have not. They are all slightly padded and – regardless of color – are allotted to holly and mistletoe alike. Perhaps a pale mistletoe berry would not have shown up on a white background.

The quilting on the original is intricate, and the maker filled every available space. While the patterns have been simplified somewhat, you may also prefer to fill every blank spot; why not, for something so special?

The quilt is neatly finished with a narrow red binding around the edges.

SIZE
Approximately 74in (188cm) square

MATERIALS REQUIRED
All fabrics 45in (115cm) wide
For the quilt top and the border: 5yds (4.6m) of white cotton
For the backing: 4½yds (3.2m) of white cotton
For the appliqué: 2¾yds (2.5m) of light green cotton, and 1yd (90cm) of dark green cotton
For the appliqué and edge binding: 1¼yds (1.2m) of red cotton
4½ yds (3.2m) of thin lightweight batting
4oz (113g) of soft polyester filling to pad the berries
Matching threads

Cut out the quilt top
All pieces are cut on the straight grain of the fabric.
Note: ¼in (6mm) seams *are* allowed for.
From the white cotton cut the pieces listed below:
9 blocks (A), each 20½in (52cm) square
2 border strips (B), each 60½in (154cm) long and

Seen in the Deming Parlour, draped over a late eighteenth-century wing chair with stop-fluted legs characteristic of Newport, is an elegant nineteenth-century quilt with a theme of Christmas love.

7¼in (18.5cm) wide, for the ends
2 border strips (C), each 74½in (188cm) long and 7¼in (18.5cm) wide, for the sides

Mark and cut the appliqué shapes
1 Trace all the templates required, and mark each one with its appropriate identification. Prepare and cut templates (see page 96).
Note: seams are *not* allowed for.
2 Leave at least ½in (12mm) between marked shapes, for seam allowances. As far as possible, mark shapes so that when they are applied their grainlines will run with those of the background fabric.
   On the dark green cotton mark 18 large holly leaves (D), and 72 smaller holly leaves (E).
   On the light green cotton mark 474 mistletoe leaves (F), comprising 378 for the hearts and 96 for the border.
   Also, marking on the bias, 18 strips (G), each 21¾in (55.25cm) long and ¾in (2cm) wide, for the outlines of the hearts (seam allowances *are* included in the width measurement for these strips).
3 On the red cotton mark 32 berries (H), each ½in (12mm) in diameter, for the border; 738 berries (I), each ⅜in (10mm) in diameter for the holly and mistletoe, and 32 swags (J) for the border.
4 Also on the red cotton, mark the red binding strips (K), 1in (2.5cm) wide, on the straight of the fabric. A total finished length of approximately 8¼yds (7.5m) will be required.
5 From the red and green fabrics, cut out all pieces D–F and J, adding a seam allowance of ¼in (6mm) around each shape. Repeat for the berries H and I.
6 Staystitch and clip curves and corners. Turn under and baste all around.
7 Also cut heart strips (G), then press seam allowances in on either side to meet at the back of each strip along the entire length.
8 Cut and join the red binding strips to make a finished length of 8¼yds (7.5m); seam allowances *are* included in the 1in (2.5cm) width.

Work the appliqué
When positioning the shapes, leave ample room for the seam allowance around each block, so that no appliqué becomes caught in the seams. Prepare each block as follows.
1 Baste or mark diagonal lines from corner to corner to aid positioning. Also mark central vertical line; mark the top and bottom points of the heart on this line. Using template G (see also template caption on page 34), draw the outline of the heart (C) on the fabric, then

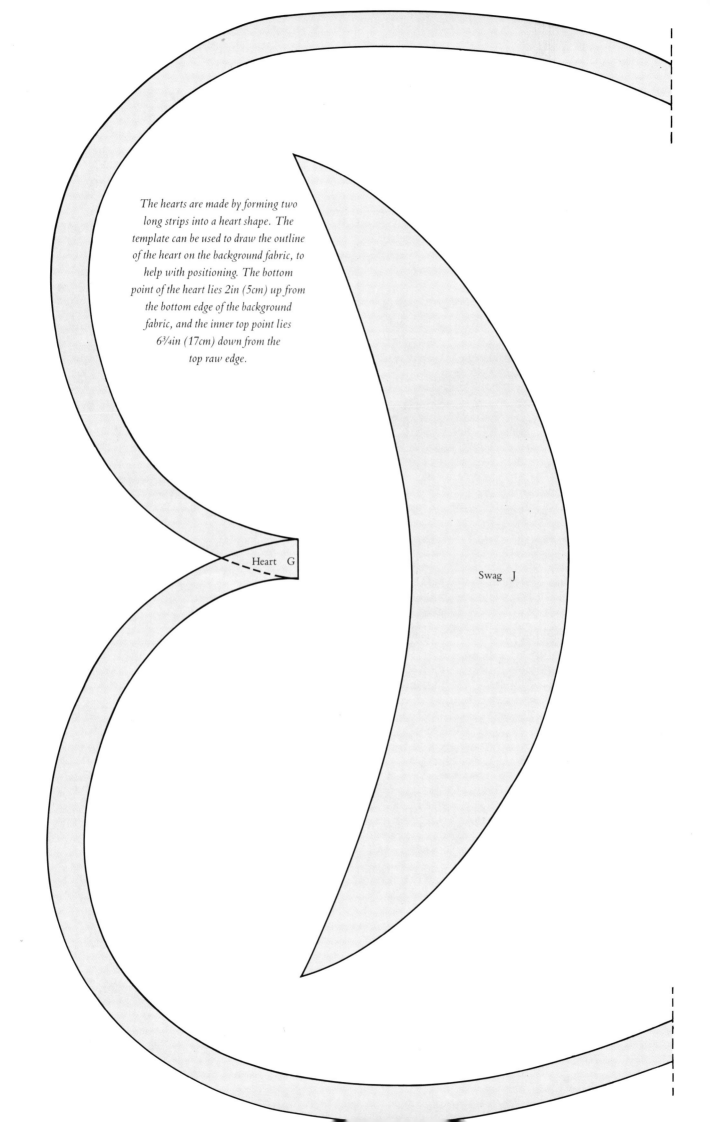

The hearts are made by forming two long strips into a heart shape. The template can be used to draw the outline of the heart on the background fabric, to help with positioning. The bottom point of the heart lies 2in (5cm) up from the bottom edge of the background fabric, and the inner top point lies 6¾in (17cm) down from the top raw edge.

Heart   G

Swag   J

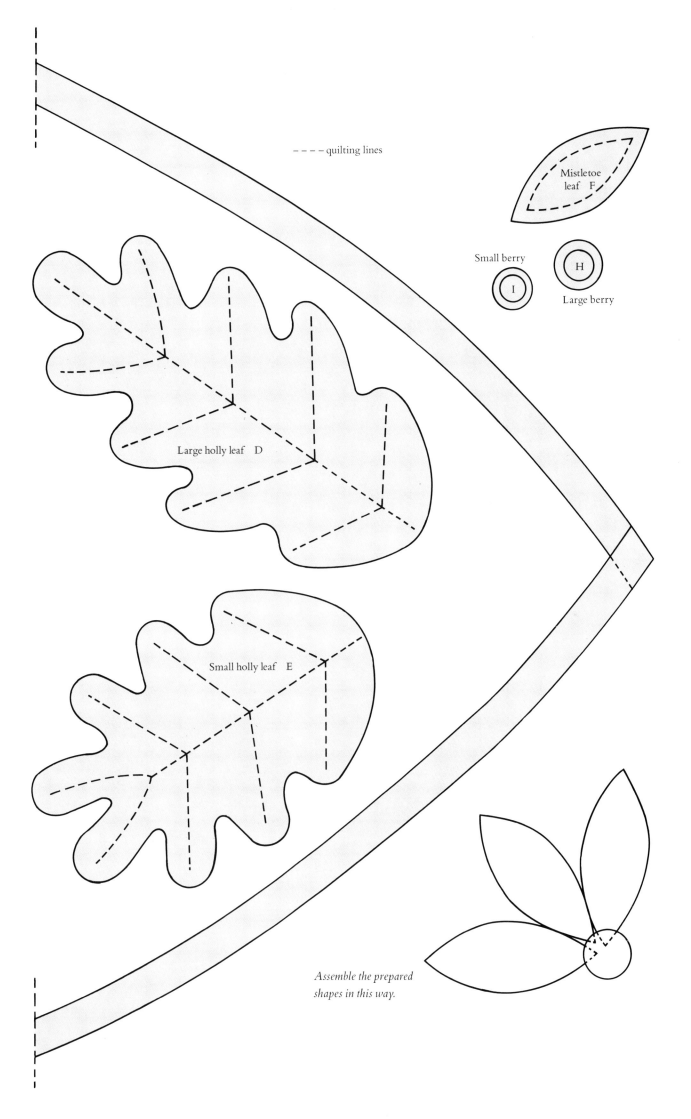

– – – – quilting lines

Mistletoe
leaf   F

Small berry

I

H

Large berry

Large holly leaf   D

Small holly leaf   E

*Assemble the prepared
shapes in this way.*

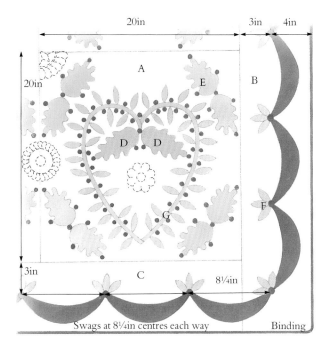

take two strips (G), and pin them in the heart shape on the fabric. With these in place, pin the rest of the shapes in position.

2 The larger holly leaves are applied in pairs within the top of the mistletoe heart; the smaller holly leaves are stitched in pairs across each corner of the block. Pin the appliqué shapes in position as follows: first the heart outline (G); then the large oak leaves in heart (D); then, inner mistletoe leaves (F); outer mistletoe leaves (F); smaller corner holly leaves (E), and lastly, working outwards from the center, the smaller red berries (I).

3 Using matching red and green threads, baste and stitch the prepared shapes into the arrangement shown in the drawing. Lap raw edges neatly under their adjacent shapes where necessary.

4 Pad the red berries (I) by tucking a little filling underneath just before you have finished stitching round them. They should not feel hard and heavy; a tiny wad about the size of a large pea is quite enough to push inside.

5 Complete the appliqué on one block, and finish off. Make the remaining eight blocks to match.

Piece the top

Note: ¼in (6mm) seams *are* allowed for.

1 Baste and stitch the trimmed blocks (A) together to make three vertical strips of three, and then join the strips to make up the nine-block square.

2 Baste and stitch the shorter border strips (B) to each of two opposite sides of the quilt. Turn under ¼in (6mm) at each end of the longer border strips (C) and baste and stitch to the two other sides.

Work the border appliqué

1 Starting at the center of one (shorter border) side, baste eight swags (J) into position, spaced to 8¼in (21cm) centers.

2 Baste three mistletoe leaves (F) where the swags meet at X, arranged as shown.

3 Baste, and pad, a red berry over the bottom ends of the leaves where they join the swags (X).

4 Stitch all around the shapes and finish the appliqué as explained on pages 97–8.

5 Repeat for the opposite border, and then for the two remaining sides of the quilt.

Quilting and finishing

1 Referring to the diagrams, mark the quilting patterns (see page 103), on the top of the quilt, as follows: the lines for outline quilting on the holly and mistletoe leaves; a feather circle round an eight-point star over the intersections of the blocks, within the holly wreaths; two plain circles within a feather circle on each of the block seamlines, between the intersections, and a rosette within each heart.

2 The border pattern on the original quilt was stitched in a running feather pattern with very little regard to the appliqué. A simplified version of this pattern is given in the quilting section (see page 103), and can be used here. Make sure that quilting lines are ¾in (2cm) clear of the raw edge of the quilt.

3 It is easier, and time-saving, to machine stitch the seams for assembling the quilt backing and batting. Cut out, join and trim the batting and the backing, so that each makes an area measuring 74in (188cm) square. Baste the completed layers of the quilt top, batting and backing together. Round off the corners slightly for easier binding.

4 Quilt along all marked lines.

5 Trim the edges of all layers to make them straight and level. Baste them firmly together near the edge, all around the quilt.

6 Bind the edges of the quilt with the strips of narrow red binding. With right sides facing, baste and stitch the binding all around the edge of the front face of the quilt, easing it around the corners. Fold binding over to the back. Turn under ¼in (6mm) all along and neatly hem down. (The binding on the original quilt was machine stitched.)

7 Press lightly.

WREATH OF ROSES

Made around the middle of the nineteenth century, this coverlet, which features a simple but very pretty interpretation of the popular Wreath of Roses design, has been enlivened with an attractive border of swags and bows. The special feature of this beautifully organized and executed piece of work is the more unusual form of quilting – padded appliqué. Not often found on bedcovers, it adds an extra dimension to the design without the risk of producing an overly heavy quilt.

All-over diamond quilting on the inner sashing serves to contain well the panels of cheerfully informal designs: and the wonderful border provides further definition of the whole – a perfect framework. While limiting the quilting on the main area, the maker worked three fine rows of trailing vine and leaves all around the borders.

SIZE
Approximately 76½in (194cm) square

MATERIALS REQUIRED
Fabrics 45in (115cm) wide, unless otherwise stated
For the top, sashing strips and borders: 4½yds (3.9m) of white bleached medium-weight cotton
For the appliqué: 1½yds (1.4m) of green cotton; 1yd (90cm) of red printed cotton, and a 12in × 10in (30cm × 25cm; scrap of orange cotton
For the backing: 4½yds (4.1m) of white cotton
To pad the appliqué: synthetic toy filling or similar soft filling
Matching threads

Cut out the quilt top
All pieces are cut with a straight edge parallel to the selvage.
Note: ¼in (6mm) seam allowances *are* allowed for.
From the white cotton, cut the pieces listed below.
   Nine blocks (A), 15in (38cm) square
   Sashing strips, all 4in (10cm) wide – six (B) 15in (38cm) long, two (C) 51in (129.5cm) long, two (D) also 51in (129.5cm) long, and two (E) 58in (147.5cm) long
   Inner border strips all 7in (17.8cm) wide – two (F) 58in (147.5cm) long, and two (G) 71in (180.5cm) long
   Outer border strips, all 3¼in (8.25cm) wide – two (H) 71in (180.5cm) long, and two (I) 76½in (194.5cm) long

Mark and cut the appliqué shapes
1 Trace all the template patterns required (see pages 41 and 104), and mark each with its appropriate identifica-tion. Prepare and cut templates (see pages 96 and 102). *Note:* seam allowances are *not* included.
2 As far as possible, mark shapes so that when they are applied their grainlines will run with those of the background fabric. Lay the templates on the fabrics and mark around them, leaving at least ½in (12mm) between shapes, for seam allowances.
   On the red cotton mark 36 roses (J), 16 bows (K), and 32 tassels (L) 16 of which should be reversed.
   On the orange cotton mark 36 rose centers (M).
   On the green cotton mark 36 stalks (N), 108 leaves (O), 12 swags (P), and 4 corner swags (Q).
3 Cut out all shapes ¼in (6mm) outside the marked line, to allow for seams.
4 Staystitch around each appliqué shape, and clip and notch curves and corners (see page 97). Turn under and baste the allowances, but leave raw edges at the ends of the stems to tuck under the roses.
5 From green cotton, cut and join strips 1in (2.5cm) wide for the edge binding, joining sufficient strips to make up a total length of 8½yds (7.75m).

Work the appliqué
1 Baste two diagonal guidelines, from corner to corner on one block (A), to help position the shapes in the design.
2 Pin the roses in position, and then the stems with the ends tucked under them, to form a circle as shown. Pin the leaves in place.
3 Blindstitch each shape to the background, inserting soft filling, a little at a time, as you work round it. Do not overpad – the applied shapes need only to be softly rounded.
4 Appliqué the eight remaining blocks to match.

Piece the top
Note: seams of ¼in (6mm) *are* allowed for.
1 With right sides facing, stitch the short sashing strips (B) to the completed blocks to form three rows of three blocks.
2 Stitch the rows together with the middle sashing strips (C), to make up the total area of blocks.
3 Add the end strips (D) to the ends, and the side strips (E) to the sides, to complete the quilt top.

This wreath of roses coverlet is made from two layers of fabric. The padding is restricted to the flowers, leaves, swags and tassels, the technique being used more for its decorative effect than for warmth.

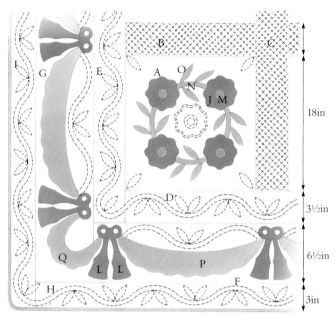

18in

3½in

6½in

3in

4 With right sides facing, join an inner border end strip (F) to each end of the quilt; then a side strip (G) to each side.

5 Join a narrow outer border end strip (H) to each of the inner borders at the ends of the quilt; then a side strip (I) to each side.

Work the border appliqué

1 Prepare the swags (P), corner swags (Q), bows (K), and tassels (L) exactly as for the shapes applied to the blocks. First pin into position the swags at the center of the sides and ends, then the remaining swags, and lastly the corner swags.

2 Next, pin on the tassels, with their tops over the intersection of the swags. Finally, pin the bows to cover the point where the tassels and swags meet.

3 If necessary, adjust the arrangement to regularize the design before basting the shapes down.

4 Blindstitch around the edges, and at the same time insert a little filling as you work.

Quilting and finishing

1 Mark the rose motif (page 104) in the center of each wreath, as shown, also the corner leaves on the blocks, and the all-over diamond pattern on the short (B) and middle sashings (C).

2 Mark three rows of the trailing vine and leaf design

(page 104): one around the side (D) and end sashings (E); a second around the inner border, inside the swags and bows appliqué; and the third around the narrow outer borders (H) and (I), outside the appliqué.

3 Cut out and join the backing pieces to make up an area 76½in (194cm) square. With right sides facing outwards, baste the completed quilt front and back together, and round off the corners.

4 Start the quilting with the center roses. Work along the marked lines, gradually working outward to the sides and corners. Quilt the inside row of vine, then the middle and lastly the outer row.

5 With right sides facing, baste and stitch the binding around the edges on the front of the quilt. Bring the binding over to the back. Turn under the ¼in (6mm) allowance and hem down, easing it around the corners.

6 Press lightly.

The template trace patterns given on the facing page include two – Swag P and Corner swag Q – that are shown half-size. To make these, fold your tracing paper; place your paper fold line to the dotted line, trace and then cut through both thicknesses of paper.

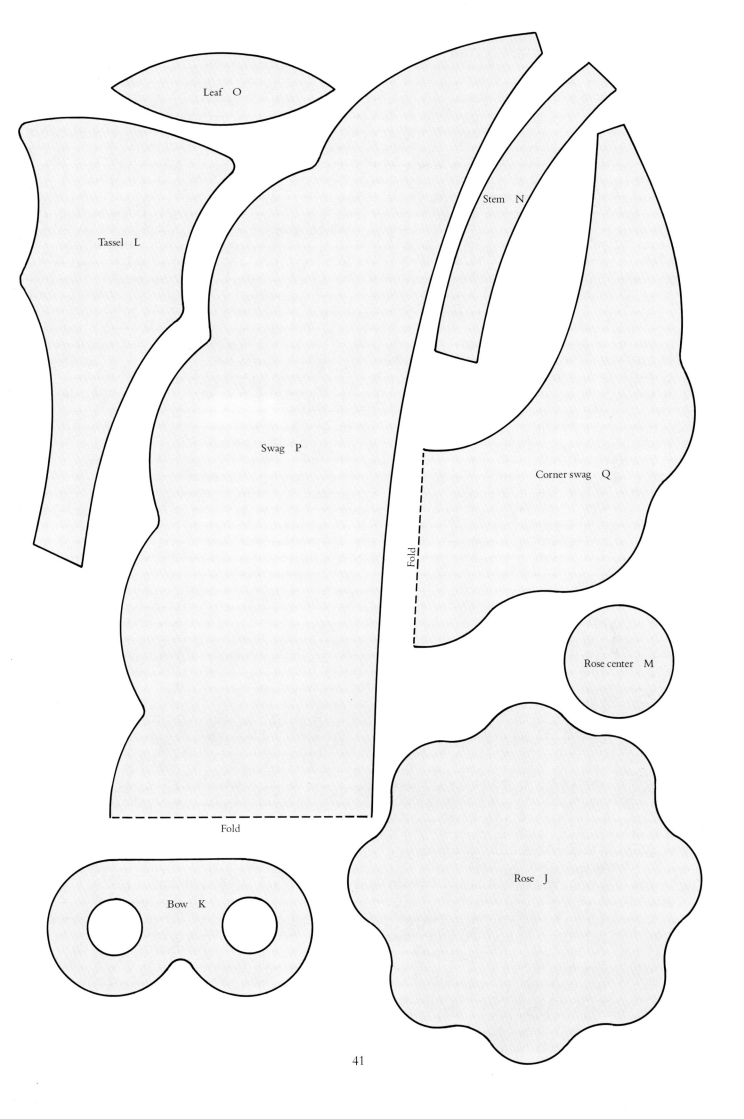

Leaf O

Tassel L

Stem N

Swag P

Corner swag Q

Fold

Rose center M

Fold

Bow K

Rose J

41

ROSE OF SHARON

The rose was a favorite motif for quilt tops and many patterns include the word 'rose' in the title. A girl often used the Rose of Sharon pattern on her bride's quilt because of the romantic association with the Song of Solomon – 'Let him kiss me with the kisses of his mouth. For thy love is better than wine. I am the Rose of Sharon and the Lily of the Valleys . . .'

This is a large quilt, and it is very pretty indeed. The lack of decoration along the top end is intriguing. Perhaps it was left plain to be slipped under the pillow to show off a beautifully embroidered pillow cover.

The rose is applied to the center of each block, with the sprays of buds and leaves fanning out towards the corners. To balance the pattern comfortably, the maker neatly arranged six blocks to face upwards to the left and six to face upwards to the right. Some thought also went into the planning of the border along the bottom end, the leaves and buds being placed vertically. The corners of the original quilt have been altered slightly for symmetry and to ensure continuity of the pattern.

The quilting is uncomplicated, no doubt to compensate for the time spent on applying such a large number of tiny pieces beforehand. Surprisingly, the quilt is edged with a binding of bright blue, a color that does not appear elsewhere in the design.

SIZE
Approximately 91½in (232.5cm) square

MATERIALS REQUIRED
All fabrics 36in (90cm) wide
For the quilt top and border: 7yds (6.4m) of lightweight, pre-shrunk, unbleached firm cotton
For the backing: 7¾yds (7.1m) of fine white cotton
For appliqué: 2¼yds (2.1m) of green printed cotton; 1¼yds (1.1m) of red printed cotton; ½yd (50cm) of pink printed cotton, and ¼yd (25cm) of plain yellow cotton
For the binding: ¼yd (25cm) of blue cotton (or use alternative, matching color, if preferred)
7¾yds (7.1m) of thin lightweight batting
Green and yellow embroidery yarns
Matching sewing threads

Made in the mid-nineteenth century, this quilt, photographed on a day bed in the Lee Room, from New Hampshire, formed part of the trousseau of Amelia Mellick, a Quaker. The charming border runs along three sides only.

Cut out the quilt top
All pieces are cut on the straight grain of the fabric.
Note: ¼in (6mm) seams *are* allowed for.
From the unbleached cotton cut the pieces listed below.
    16 blocks (A), each 16½in (42cm) square
    2 border strips (B), each 10¼in (26cm) wide and 72in (183cm) long, for the ends of the quilt.
    2 border strips (C), each 10¼in (26cm) wide and 91½in (232.5cm) long, for the sides
    From the blue cotton cut out the binding for the edges. A total finished length of about 10¼yds (9.36m), 1in (2.5cm) wide, will be required.

Mark and cut the appliqué shapes
1 Trace all the template patterns required (see page 44) and mark each one with its correct identification. Prepare and cut templates (see page 96).
Note: seam allowances are *not* included on the appliqué templates.
2 Mark shapes so that when they are applied their grainlines will run with those of the background fabric.
    Lay the templates on the fabric and mark around them, leaving at least ½in (12mm) between each shape, for adding seam allowances.
    On the red cotton mark 16 outer rose shapes (D), and 196 buds (E).
    On the yellow cotton mark 16 rose centers (G).
    On the green cotton mark 16 rose stems (H), 196 calyces (I), 204 leaves (J), 112 shorter rosebud stems (K), 84 longer rosebud stems (L).
3 From the red, pink, yellow and green fabrics, cut out all shapes (D-L), adding a seam allowance of ¼in (6mm) around each shape. Staystitch around each shape, and clip around curves and into corners. Turn under and baste all edges (see page 97).
4 From remaining green cotton, mark bias strips ¾in (2cm) wide and up to 36in (90cm) long, to join for the trailing creeper (M). A total length of approximately 8½yds (7.75m) will be required. Press seams in on either side to meet down the centre back.

Cut the sashing strips
Note: seams *are* allowed for.
On the green cotton, mark the sashing strips, all 2in (5cm) wide: 12 short horizontal (N), each 16½in (42cm) long, for joining the blocks; 3 vertical (O), each 69in (175.5cm) long, for joining the rows of blocks; 2 horizontal (P), each 69in (175.5cm) long, for the ends; and 2 vertical (Q), each 72in (183cm) long, for the sides. Cut out all the sashing strips.

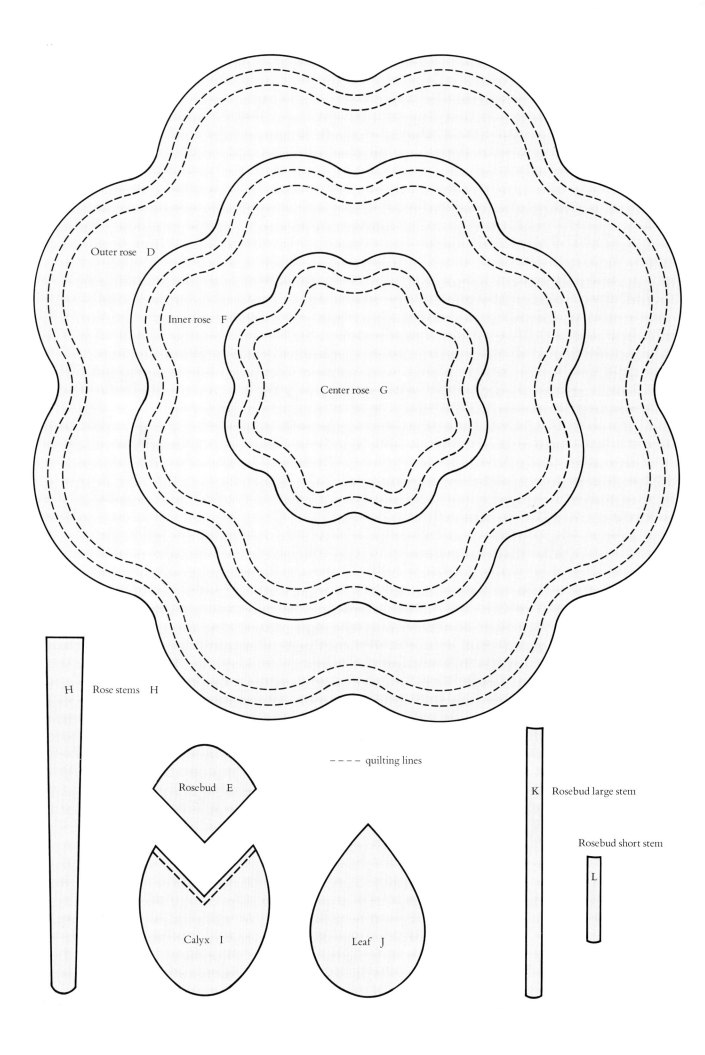

Outer rose D

Inner rose F

Center rose G

Rose stems H

– – – – quilting lines

Rosebud E

Rosebud large stem

Rosebud short stem

Calyx I

Leaf J

Work the appliqué

Baste diagonal guidelines for positioning the appliqué design from corner to corner across a block, and arrange the design according to the drawing.

1 First pin the layers (D,F,G) of the rose to the center of the block. Then tuck the ends of the rose stalk and rosebud stems under the edges of the rose, and the leaves and calyces on to the other ends of the stems. Pin all these elements in place. The raw edges at the lower ends of the buds tuck under the calyces.

2 Baste and stitch down the positioned shapes, using matching threads. Finish off the appliqué as explained on pages 97–8.

3 Embroider the stems of the leaves in chain stitch, using green yarn.

4 With the yellow yarn, embroider three stamens in chain stitch at the end of every rosebud, making each stamen about ¾in (2cm long).

5 Appliqué and embroider the remaining fifteen blocks to match.

Piece the top

Note: ¼in (6mm) turnings *are* allowed for.

1 With right sides facing, stitch the 12 short green horizontal strips (N) to the 16 blocks (A) to make four rows of four blocks each. Make sure that each rose faces the correct way (see diagram).

2 Join the rows of blocks together with the three strips (O), then add a horizontal strip (P) to each end. Finally, add a strip (Q) to each side.

3 Stitch the two shorter border strips (B) across each end. Add on the two side stips (C).

Work the border appliqué

Note that the top end of the quilt is undecorated.

1 Join the strips for the creeper to make a sufficient length to trail in a wavy line along two sides and one end of the border.

2 Fold the length of the creeper in half across the width to find the central point, and pin this (unfolded) to the center of the bottom border. Following the layout shown in the drawing, pin the creeper, in a wavy line, out toward each corner, and then up the sides. Position the curves so that they fall evenly on either side of the midway point of the border width.

3 Tuck the raw ends of all the leaf and calyx stems under the edges of the creeper, and pin them in place.

4 When the design all around the border is satisfactorily arranged, baste and stitch the appliqué. Finish as instructed on pages 97–8.

5 Embroider the small stems of the pairs of leaves on

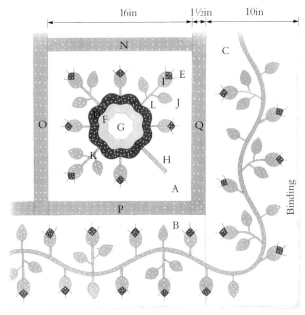

Chain-stitched stamens to all rosebuds

Bottom of quilt

Notice the lines indicating the chain-stitched stamens at the end of each rosebud.

the bud stems in chain stitch, using green yarn.

6 In yellow yarn, embroider three chain stitch stamens, each ¾in (2cm) long, at the end of every rosebud.

Quilting and finishing

1 On the right side of the quilt top, mark the quilting lines on each layer of the large roses. Mark diagonal lines, ½in (12mm) apart, each way across the quilt top for the diamond pattern; do not mark across the large roses – only to their edges.

2 Cut out and join the batting pieces and backing so that each makes an area measuring 91½in (232cm) square. Baste the completed layers of the quilt top, batting and backing together (see page 108).

3 Quilt along all marked lines.

4 Round off the corners slightly for easier binding. Trim around the edges of all layers to make them straight and level. Baste the edges of the layers firmly together.

5 Join the blue binding strips for the edge to make a binding 10¼yds (9.36m) long. With right sides facing, baste and stitch it all around the edges on to the front face of the quilt. Fold it over to the back and turn under the ¼in (6mm) allowance. Hem neatly down and press lightly.

PIECED QUILTS

THE FIRST PIECED QUILTS were nearly always of geometric shapes. These made the most economical use of fabric, and straight lines were easy to sew with a simple running stitch. On pieced blocks, the quilting sometimes merely follows the outline of the geometric shape, but when these alternate with blocks of a solid color, there is usually intricate quilting on the plain fabric.

From about 1830 onward, patterns for geometric quilt blocks were published in American women's magazines, and by the middle of the century, the design-

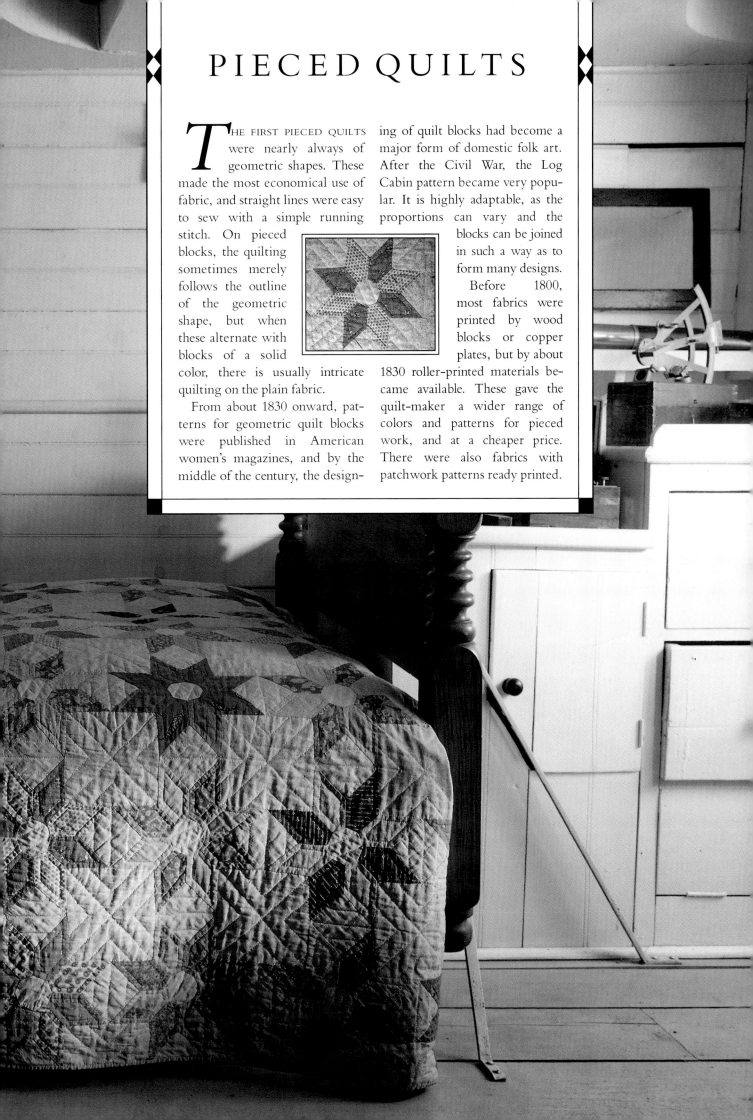

ing of quilt blocks had become a major form of domestic folk art. After the Civil War, the Log Cabin pattern became very popular. It is highly adaptable, as the proportions can vary and the blocks can be joined in such a way as to form many designs.

Before 1800, most fabrics were printed by wood blocks or copper plates, but by about 1830 roller-printed materials became available. These gave the quilt-maker a wider range of colors and patterns for pieced work, and at a cheaper price. There were also fabrics with patchwork patterns ready printed.

STARS AND OCTAGONS

No less than 35 different printed cottons have been worked into this delightful coverlet to create a glorious jewel-studded effect. Octagons are less used than hexagons, as the former are difficult to fit in with other geometric shapes. The top is pieced with diamonds and triangles, the octagons being applied to the centres of the diamond 'flowers'. If carefully cut and well-aligned, the piecing can be worked with a sewing machine.

SIZE
Approximately 85in × 75½in (216cm × 192cm)

MATERIALS REQUIRED
All fabrics 45in (115cm) wide
For the octagons, and for small and large triangles:
3¼yds (3m) of white or cream cotton
For diamonds: 3yds (2.74m) *in total* of 17 different pale and 17 dark-colored cotton prints
For backing and binding: 4¼yds (3.89m) of cotton print
4¾yds (4.4m) of lightweight polyester batting
Matching threads.

Marking and cutting
1 Draw the four templates to full scale on graph paper. Paste the shapes to cardboard and cut out (see page 100).
2 Mark the fabric on the wrong side, leaving at least ½in (12mm) between each shape, for seam allowances (marked lines are seamlines). One side of each triangle and one side of each octagon should lie on the straight grain of the fabric.

In matching sets of four, mark 288 diamonds (A) on the pale and 288 on the dark prints. On the white fabric, mark 576 triangles (B), and 576 small triangles (C).
3 Also on white fabric, but marking on the *right* side, mark 72 octagons (D).
4 Cut out all shapes, adding ¼in (6mm) seams all around.
5 From the backing fabric, cut and join binding strips 1in (2.5cm) wide (seams *are* included), to make a total length of 9yds (8.25m).

Piece the top
Join pieces along the marked lines, with right sides

The unusual quilt on the preceding page, made in 1850, is draped over the bed of the captain's cabin, reproduced from the whaling ship Charles W. Morgan.

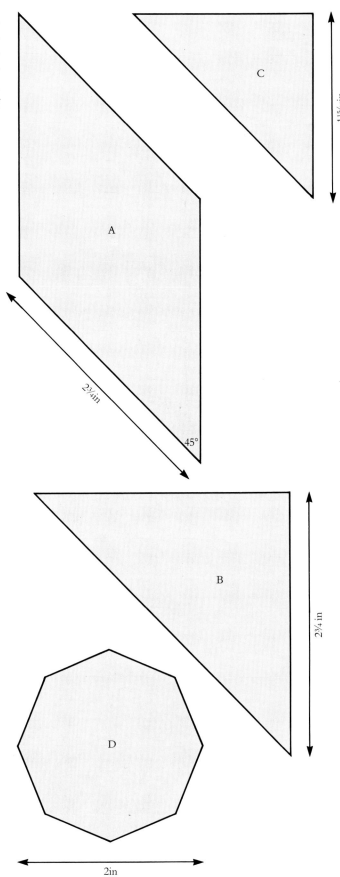

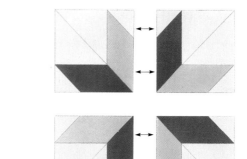

facing. Each of the 72 blocks consists of four smaller blocks, with one pale and one dark diamond in each.

1 To make a block, start by joining a diamond to a triangle (B), and continue as shown in the diagram. Next, turn under the edges of an octagon and appliqué it to the center matching octagon corners to diamond seams.

2 To avoid a lump at the center, cut excess fabric away from behind the appliqué shape.

3 With right sides facing, join finished blocks to make eight strips of nine blocks, then join strips.

Finishing the coverlet

1 Join batting and backing so that each makes an area 85in × 75½in (216cm × 192cm) and, with wrong sides facing, baste the layers together.

2 Quilt with outline quilting inside the diamonds and with straight lines, as shown in the photograph.

3 When quilting is complete, trim and level the edges, baste the edges together and bind with the prepared strips, as for the quilt on page 16.

STRIPPY

A strippy quilt was always made with an odd number of strips. The strips might be of whole cloth, or pieced, or a combination of both; sometimes, as in this example, where a bright blue chintz is used, the center strip was slightly different from the others.

The fabrics used for this quilt are mainly European glazed chintzes of the late eighteenth century. The backing is of homespun linen, and the edge has been bound with a hand-woven tape.

SIZE
Approximately 105in × 91in (267cm × 228cm)

MATERIALS REQUIRED
All fabrics 48in (122cm) wide
For the pieced squares: 1⅜yds (1.3m) in total of dark cotton prints and 1⅛ yds (1m) pale cotton prints
For triangles: ½yd (46cm) of bright blue printed glazed chintz (central pieced strip); 1½yds (1.4m) light blue printed glaze chintz (other pieced strips)
For unpieced strips: 3yds (2.75m) of brown, blue and cream printed glazed chintz
For backing: 6yds (5.5m) of plain cotton
6yds (5.5m) of polyester or cotton batting
For binding: 11¼yds (10.3m) purchased bias binding
Matching threads

Marking and cutting
1 Draw the templates to full scale on graph paper. Paste the shapes to cardboard and cut out (see page 100).
2 Mark the fabric on the wrong side, leaving at least ½in (12mm) between each shape, for seam allowances (marked lines are seamlines). Position templates with marked grainlines matching that of the fabrics.
3 Mark 275 squares (A) on dark prints and 220 on pale fabrics; 20 triangles (B) on bright blue and 80 on light blue chintz, and 4 triangles (C) on bright blue and 16 on light blue chintz.
4 Cut out all shapes, adding ¼in (6mm) seams all around.
5 Cutting on the straight grain, cut six strips 7½in x 105½in (19cm × 268cm) from the brown chintz.

Initialled in cross stitch on the reverse of this quilt is 'S.G. 1817'. The 'cedar' grained pine panels seen in the background come from the parlor of a house built in 1763 by Captain William Perley, who commanded his men at the Battle of Bunker Hill.

Piece the top
1 Alternating prints of light and dark colors as shown in the assembly diagrams above and overleaf, make 55 blocks, joining three rows of three squares for each.
2 Starting by joining triangle C to a pieced block, make the pieced strips, as shown in the diagrams.
3 With right sides facing, stitch the pieced and brown strips together, putting the bright blue strip in the center. Press seams.

Quilting and finishing
1 Cut and join batting and backing, so that each measures 105in × 90in (267cm × 229cm). Baste the three layers together (see page 108).
2 Quilt as shown in the photograph (all quilting lines are ¾in (2cm) apart).
3 Trim the edges to neaten them. Round off the corners and baste around the edges. Attach the binding as for the quilt on page 16.

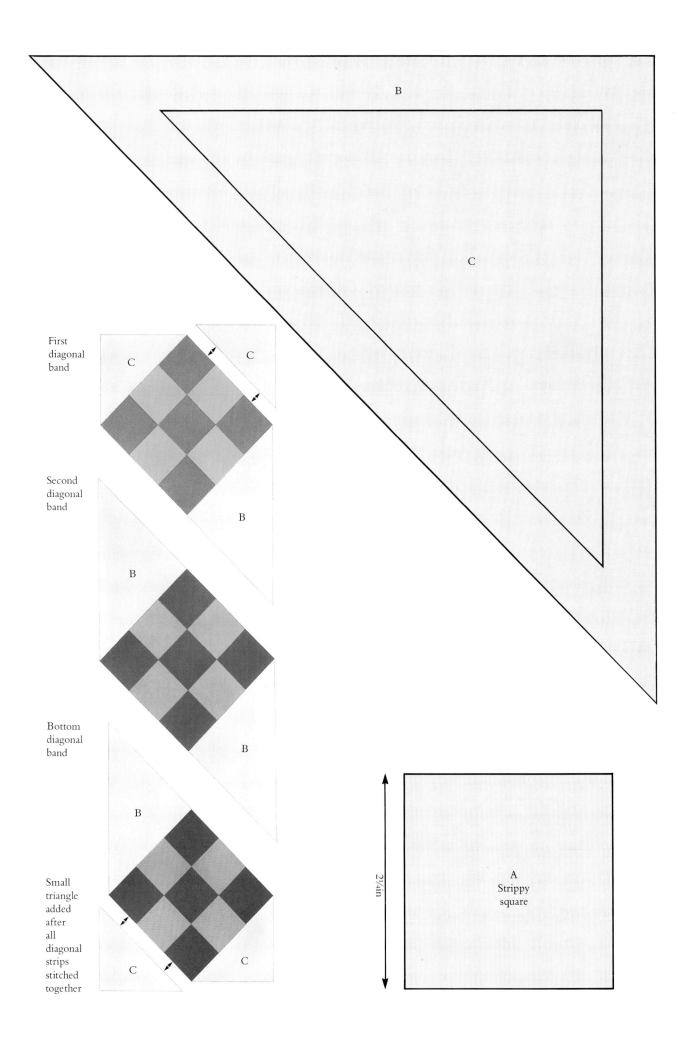

B

C

First
diagonal
band

C

C

Second
diagonal
band

B

B

Bottom
diagonal
band

B

B

Small
triangle
added
after
all
diagonal
strips
stitched
together

B

C

C

2¼in

A
Strippy
square

SILK SQUARES THROW

The maker of this luxurious silk throw knew what she was doing when she devised such a remarkable piece of work. The combination of wonderfully rich textures and radiant colors is superb. The collection of silks and brocades used indicates that they were probably scraps left from ball gowns and best gowns made for herself and her family and friends. Although the throw is lightly padded, it has not been quilted.

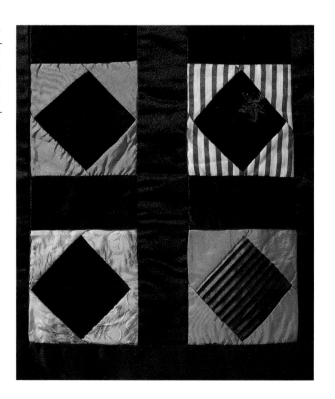

SIZE
Approximately 55in × 50in (140cm × 127cm)

MATERIALS REQUIRED
All fabrics except those used for the pieced squares are 36in (90cm) wide

For the pieced squares – this is a true scrap-bag piece, and only small quantities of fabrics are required: 3¼in (8.3cm) squares for each center square, and 4¼in (10.8cm) squares for each set of four surrounding triangles

For sashing strips C and D: 1½yds (1.4m) of black satin

For the border: 1yd (90cm) of deep maroon satin

For the backing: 3¼yds (3m) of gold-colored watered silk

3¼yds (3m) of thin, lightweight polyester or cotton batting

Threads to match the fabrics

C
Silk Squares
Throw
sashing
strip

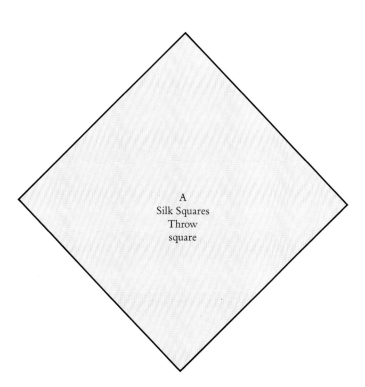

A
Silk Squares
Throw
square

B
Silk Squares
Throw
triangle

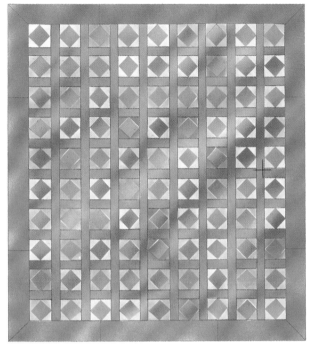

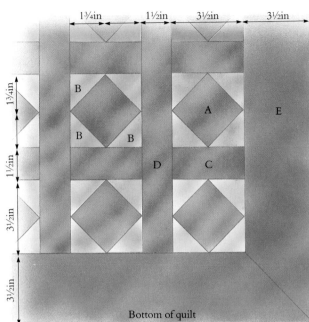

Marking and cutting

1 Draw templates A, B and C to full scale on graph paper. Paste the paper to cardboard and cut out the template shapes (see page 100).

2 For all pieces (A-G), mark the fabric on the *wrong* side, leaving at least ½in (12mm) between each shape, for seam allowances (marked lines are seamlines). Position templates with right angles matching the grainlines of the fabrics.

On piecework fabrics, mark 90 squares (A), and 90 sets of four triangles (B). On black satin, mark 81 sashing strips (C).

3 Also on black satin, mark eight long sashing strips (D), each 49in × 2in (124.5cm × 5cm).

4 On maroon satin, mark 3¼in (8.3cm)-wide border strips: eight (E), 15in (38cm) long; two (F), 20in (51cm) long, and two (G), 25in (63.5cm) long.

5 Cut out marked shapes, adding ¼in (6mm) seams all around.

Piece the top

1 With right sides facing, join long sides of four triangles, one by one, to the sides of a square. Complete 90 blocks.

2 Join short sashing strips (C) to blocks to make nine rows of ten, then join these with long strips (D).

Finishing the throw

1 Cut and join lengths of batting and backing until each measures 55in × 50in (140cm × 127cm).

2 With the batting in the middle and the pieced top centered over the other two, baste the three layers together (see page 108).

3 Make the border frame: join two end strips in order E-F-E, and two side strips in order E-G-E. Baste and stitch the strips together with mitred corners, snipping inner and outer corners.

4 With right sides together, and stitching through all layers, join the inner border frame to the pieced top.

5 Fold the border over to the back, turn in the edge, and slipstitch to the backing.

A richly-glowing throw of pieced silks and satins, backed with gold silk, and made around 1880, is draped over an early piano in the Greek Revival Room. Unpadded, a throw of this type is likely to have been made for use in the parlor rather than the bedroom.

DOLL'S QUILT

Little girls have always been interested in making clothing and bedcovers for their dolls. The *American Girls' Book*, published in 1831, remarks, 'Little girls often find amusement in making patchwork quilts for the beds of their dolls, and some even go so far as to make cradle quilts for their infant brothers and sisters.' The backing is of white cotton with a red sprig.

SIZE
Approximately 19½in (49cm) square

MATERIALS REQUIRED
For alternate squares: plain white cotton, 36in (90cm) wide
For the colored squares, scraps of fabric, as follows:
Fabrics a and b – 12in × 8in (30cm × 20cm) of deep blue and of brown print; **c** – 12in × 6in (30cm × 15cm) of blue spotted print; **d** – 8in (20cm) square of plain pink; **e** – 8in × 6in (20cm × 15cm) of pink dot print; **f** – 8in × 4in (20cm × 10cm) of pink print; **g** – 4in (10cm) square of blue-and-pink print
For the borders: 9in (23cm) of blue chevron print, 36in (90cm) wide; 18in × 8in (45cm × 20cm) of yellow print, and 6in (15cm) square of flower print
For the backing: 21in (53cm) square of white-and-pink sprigged print

Marking and cutting
1 Draw two templates on graph paper: one 1in (2.5cm) square (A), and one 1½in (4cm) square (B). Paste the shapes to cardboard and cut out (see page 100).
2 Mark the fabric on the wrong side, leaving ½in (12mm) between shapes, for seam allowance.

Using template A mark pieces as follows: **a** 28, **b** 24, **c** 20, **d** 16, **e** 12, **f**, 8, and **g** 4, and 113 squares on white fabric.

Also, with template B, cut four (border corner) pieces from the flower print.

For the border, mark on blue chevron fabric: four strips (C) 1¼in × 15½in (3.2cm × 39.5cm), and four (D) 1¼in × 20in (3.2cm × 51cm). On yellow print,

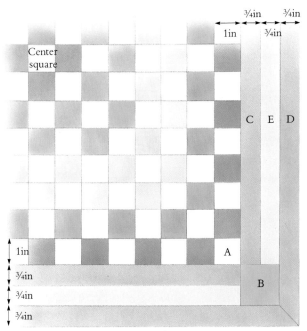

Bottom of quilt

mark four strips (E) 1¼in x 15½in (3.2cm × 39.5cm).
For the backing, mark a 20in (51cm) square (F).
3 Cut out all pieces, adding a ¼in (6mm) seam allowance around each.

Piece the top
1 Following the color arrangement seen in the photograph, and with right sides facing, piece the top. Make 15 strips of 15 squares (A). Press all seams. Join the strips into one square. Press seams.
2 With right sides together, stitch two border strips (C and E) together, lengthwise. Repeat, to make three more double strips. Stitch one strip to each side of the pieced square (blue edge next to the square). Stitch a corner (B) to each end of the remaining strips, then join these to the coverlet. Stitch the outer border strips around the edges, mitring corners.

Finishing
1 Turn in the edges ¼in (6mm) and baste. Turn in the edges of the backing and baste. With wrong sides together, baste the top and backing together, ready for quilting (see page 108).
2 Quilt in an all-over diamond pattern across the coverlet, setting the lines ¾in (2cm) apart.
3 Neatly blindstitch the edges together.

AMISH SHOO-FLY

Amish quilts are usually non-representational, and patterned fabrics are forbidden, but Midwest quilts are sometimes named after block designs, such as Shoo-fly, created by the 'English', as all non-Amish people are called. This striking quilt is pieced in fine wool with a polished cotton background.

SIZE

Approximately 85¼in × 71in (216cm × 180.5cm)

MATERIALS REQUIRED

Use batting and backing fabric 36in (90cm) wide; all other fabrics, 45in (115cm) wide
For the pieced work and border: 4yds (3.7m) of black glazed cotton
For pieced work: ¾yd (70cm) brown cotton, and ½yd (50cm) cream cotton or wool/cotton mixture
For the inner border: ½yd (50cm) beige cotton or wool/cotton mixture
For the backing: 5yds (4.6m) black cotton
5yds (4.6m) polyester or soft cotton batting
Matching threads

Marking and cutting

1 Draw templates on graph paper, marking grainlines; paste the graph paper to card and cut out (see page 100).
2 Mark the fabric on the *wrong* side, leaving ½in (12mm) between shapes, for seams.

Mark and cut pieces as follows. From black cotton cut 20 of template A; 80 B; 80 C; 12 plain blocks (D); 14 E, and 4 F. From brown cotton cut 144 C and 48 G, and from cream cotton 96 C and 32 G.
3 Cut border strips 5½in (14cm) wide (this includes the seams) from black fabric, two pieces 60½in (154cm) long, for the ends, and two 85¼in (216) long, for sides.
4 Cut inner borders, 2½in (6.4cm) wide from beige: two 56½in (143.5cm) for the ends, and two 75¼in (191cm) for the sides.

Piece the top

1 With right sides together, piece blocks. Join three triangles (C) – cream, black inverted, cream – then join this strip to a large triangle (B). Add a cream C to complete the square. Make a second square, and join the two with a cream rectangle (G). Repeat, and then join two cream G shapes with an A at the center. Join the three strips together to complete the block. Make 12 brown-and-black and 8 cream-and-black blocks.
2 Join blocks in diagonal rows, alternating pieced blocks with solid black squares and completing the

Top of quilt

strips either with triangles (E) at the ends, or with F triangles, at the corners.
3 Join the strips, adding the two remaining corner triangles to complete the pieced area.
4 Stitch a short beige strip to each end, then stitch the longer strips to the sides. Add the black border strips in the same order of sequence.

Quilting and finishing

1 Mark the quilting design (see overleaf) on the face: horizontal lines, 1in (2.5cm) apart on pieced blocks; circular flower pattern on black blocks and tulip-and-leaf design on black side triangles (trace these on folded paper, to make whole templates) hour-glass design around beige border, and rambling tulip-and-leaf around black border.
2 Cut and join batting and backing so that each measures 85¼in × 71in (216cm × 180.5cm).
3 Baste the layers together (see page 108), and then quilt.
4 Trim the batting back by ½in (12mm) all around. Fold the edge of the front over the batting, then turn in the raw edge of the backing; the latter should be about ⅛ in (3mm) inside the edge of the front. Neatly hem stitch all around.

Made in Milton, Iowa, in 1929, this is
a typical Amish quilt, made in austere,
plain colors with strong contrast.

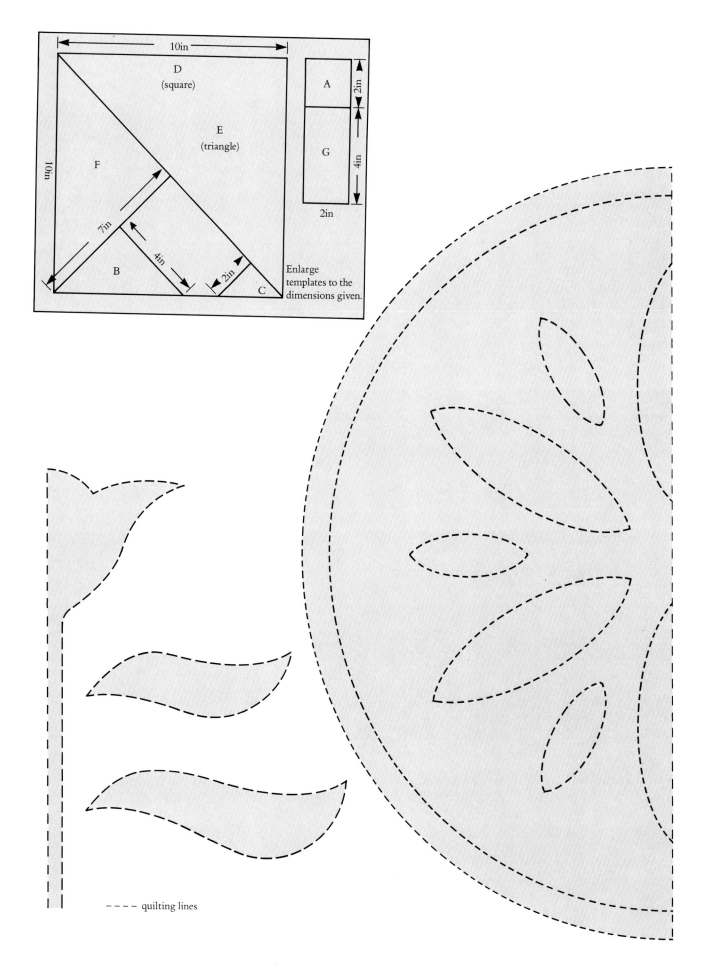

D
(square)

10in

E
(triangle)

10in

F

7in

A

2in

G

4in

2in

B

4in

2in

C

Enlarge
templates to the
dimensions given.

- - - - quilting lines

SAILBOATS

With its jaunty little boats sailing off in all directions, this is an enchanting crib cover to make for the youngest member of the family. The 'boats' are made with one-half of the block known as Swallow, and the sawtooth border and matching narrow binding give an attractive finish to this nursery quilt.

SIZE
Approximately 42½in × 38in (108cm × 96cm)

MATERIALS REQUIRED
All fabrics 45in (115cm) wide
For pieced work and border: 1½yds (1.4m) of white cotton
For pieced work and binding: ¾yd (70cm) of red cotton print
For the backing: 1¼yds (1.15m) of white or coordinating cotton print
1¼yd (1.15m) of lightweight cotton batting
Matching threads

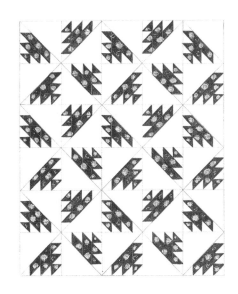

Marking and cutting

1 Trace the templates on graph paper, marking grainlines; paste the graph paper to cardboard and cut out the templates (see page 100).

2 Mark the fabric on the wrong side, leaving ½in (12mm) between shapes, for seams.

Mark and cut pieces as follows: on the white cotton, mark triangles – 30 A, 102 B and 210 C; on red cotton print, mark 102 B and 270 C. Cut out, adding ¼in (6mm) all around.

3 On red print, mark and cut strips, 1in (2.5cm) wide, and join them to make a total length of 4½yds (4.1m).

4 From white cotton, cut border strips: two for the ends (D), 25½in × 5in (65cm × 12.7cm), and two for the sides (E), 39½in × 5¼in (100.5cm × 13.3cm).

Piece the top

1 With right sides facing, and inverting every alternate triangle to produce a straight row, piece a block. Start with a row of triangles (B) – one white, five red and one white – then work out to the corner, making progres-

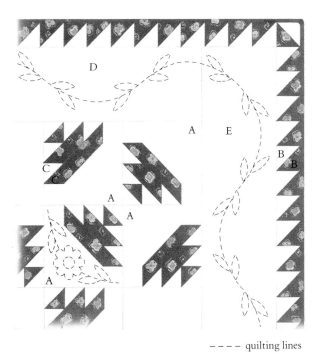

- - - - quilting lines

The brightly-colored quilt, made around 1845, lies over a crib in the Borning Room. A small guest chamber, situated near the kitchen, this was often used in time of childbirth, hence the name. It also served during illness and was sometimes called the 'measles' room.

sively shorter rows. Join these to make a half block, then add a large white triangle (A) to complete the block. Make 29 more blocks.

2 Noting the direction in which the boats face on the drawing, make five rows of six blocks, then join these together to complete the top.

3 With right sides facing, stitch a border strip (D) to each end, then add the side strips (E).

4 Noting the direction of the teeth, piece alternate red and white triangles (B), making two strips of sawtooth border for the ends. Attach these and then, paying particular attention to the corners, make two strips for the sides. Attach these also.

5 The quilting patterns are simple, and many of those given in the book would be suitable. Mark a rose-and-leaf quilting pattern on each large white triangle, and mark a trailing vine pattern around the plain white border.

Quilting and finishing

1 Cut and join backing and batting so that each measures the same as the pieced top. Assemble the layers together and baste (see page 108).

2 Stitching along each side of every triangle, outline quilt the boats and surrounding white triangles. Also stitch the marked quilting patterns.

3 Round off the corners and baste the layers of the quilt together around the edges. With right sides facing and taking a ¼in (6mm) seam, baste and stitch the binding to the front of the quilt (see page 16). Fold it over the back, making a ¼in (6mm) hem, and neatly sew.

The border of the original quilt was inaccurately made, with the triangles changing direction. To work the bottom border, alternate red and white triangles so that the long sides lie on a north-east/south-west axis. As you proceed up the left-hand side the axis changes to north-west/south-east. Continue as shown.

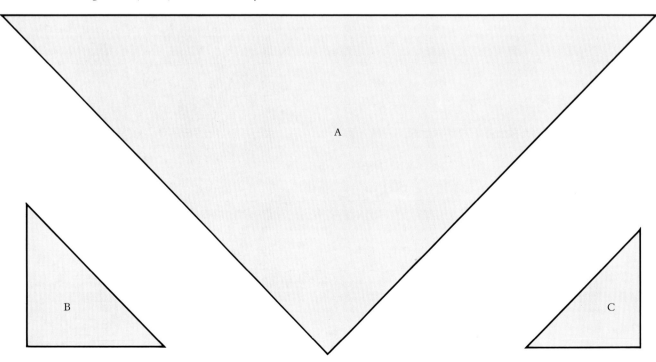

LOG CABIN COVERLET

This elegant silk coverlet was made by Lucy Chapin Hawley and her mother and sisters while her father was away fighting in the Civil War. Very skillfully, they used pieces from their dresses to create a dramatic arrangement of rich colors and textures. The coverlet is backed with finely woven red wool, and the tied method of quilting is used to hold the layers together. Each knot is charmingly concealed at the back with a tiny blue satin bow.

Although log cabin blocks can be joined by machine, the strips used here are so narrow that, except for very experienced machinists, most people would find them easier to stitch by hand.

SIZE
Approximately 63in (160cm) square

MATERIALS REQUIRED
All fabrics 36in (90cm) wide
For the log cabin strips: a total of 4yds (3.6m) of light-colored silks and brocades and the same of dark-colored ones
For the centre squares: ½yd (50cm) of black velvet
For foundation squares: 3¾yds (3.4m) of fine cotton (this is not essential for all log cabin work, but will help in this case to eliminate tension between differing fabrics and keep the work in good shape)
For the backing: 3¾yds (3.4m) of fine wool or wool/cotton mixture
For the front border and corners: velvet ribbon, 2in (5cm) wide – 7½yds (6.9m) in a plum color, and ⅝yd (60cm) in brown
For back border and back corner bows: 8½yds (7.8m) of blue satin ribbon, 2in (5cm) wide, and 14yds (12.8m) of blue satin ribbon, ¼in (6mm) wide
For tying: embroidery yarn or crochet cotton

Marking and cutting

1 Draw templates on graph paper – template A is 1½in (3.8cm) square and template B is 6½in (16.5cm) square. Paste the shapes to cardboard and cut out (see page 100).
2 Mark the fabric on the wrong side, leaving ½in (12mm) between shapes, for seams.

Mark 100 center squares (A) on black velvet and 100 foundation squares (B) on fine cotton; add ¼in (6mm) around each marked shape, and cut out.
3 Similarly, mark and cut strips ⅜in (8mm) wide and up to 18in (45cm) long on the straight grain of silks, adding ¼in (6mm) all around.

Piece the top

Whether you work clockwise or counter-clockwise, it is essential to work in the same direction throughout. All stitching must pass through the foundation fabric. Each block is made as follows.
1 Draw diagonal lines from corner to corner across a cotton square (B). Use the lines to center a velvet square (A), right side up, on the cotton. Baste to secure.

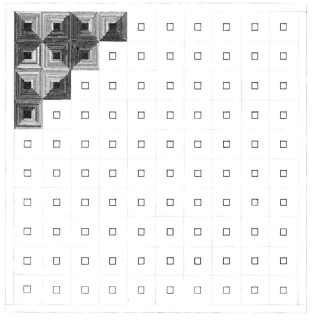

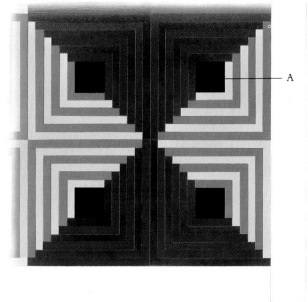

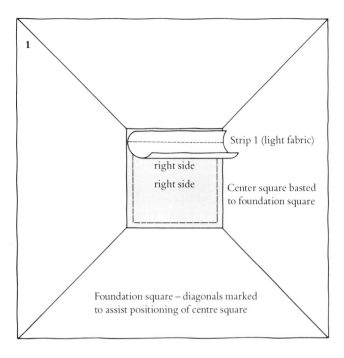

1

Strip 1 (light fabric)

right side

right side

Center square basted
to foundation square

Foundation square – diagonals marked
to assist positioning of centre square

2 Take a light-colored strip; trim it to size and, with right sides facing, baste and stitch it to one side of the square. Fold outwards and press flat. Take a second, identical, light strip, stitch it down the next side of the square and along the end of the first strip. The third and fourth strips are dark. Continue in this way, always ending with the longest dark strip, until you have attached six strips to each side.

3 Complete a total of 100 blocks, and trim away the excess foundation fabric around each.

4 Join four blocks so that the all-dark corners meet at the centre. Make 19 further sets of four; following the diagram, join them in strips and then join the strips.

Tying and finishing

1 Cut and join pieces of backing fabric to make an area the same as the top. With wrong sides facing, baste the two together and trim the edges.

2 Cut four strips of plum ribbon, one for each edge of the throw. With right sides facing, attach one to each end. Then cut four 2¼in (6cm) lengths of brown ribbon and attach one to each end of the two remaining lengths of plum ribbon, and attach these to the remaining sides. Turn the ribbon under by ¼in (6mm) all around the edge; baste and then slipstitch.

3 Starting at one corner at the back, baste wide blue ribbon around the edges, ⅛in (3mm) in from the turned edge of the plum ribbon and covering the slipstitching. Mitre the corners and turn the end of the ribbon under to mitre the final corner. Herringbone the outer edge to the plum ribbon. The inner edge is also herringboned.

4 Tie the quilt (see page 109): mark the positions of the knots with a marker or thread pulled through. Working from the back, make a tie knot at the intersections of the blocks (except the border). Make 81 small bows from narrow blue ribbon and stitch one to each knot, at the back of the throw. Make four larger bows from the remaining wide blue ribbon and stitch one to each back corner, in the inner angle of the mitres.

Strip 1 folded out and pressed flat

2

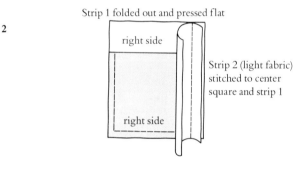

right side

Strip 2 (light fabric)
stitched to center
square and strip 1

right side

3

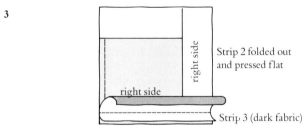

right side

Strip 2 folded out
and pressed flat

right side

Strip 3 (dark fabric)

4

Strip 4 (dark fabric)

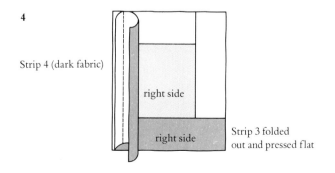

right side

right side

Strip 3 folded
out and pressed flat

*The sheen and lustre of jewel-colored
silks are displayed in this strongly
contrasting Log Cabin design. Made in
the 1860s, almost certainly as a sofa
throw, it is shown in the late eighteenth-
century setting of the Deer Park
Parlor.*

PIECED AND APPLIQUE QUILTS

URING THE EIGHT-EENTH CENTURY, very few quilts were entirely pieced. It was more usual to piece the central portion only, and surround it with an appliqué border. One of the most popular borders was 'swags and bows', the bows being worked in many different shapes. Sometimes the swags alternated with tassels.

A single block might contain both pieced work and appliqué; the pattern would be pieced, while details, such as the contents of the baskets in basket quilts, would be applied to the pieced pattern. In other cases, stems and leaves were applied to complete a pieced design.

In contrast, a quilt which is mainly appliqué can be enhanced by pieced borders. Many of the Baltimore Album quilts have pieced outer borders and sashing strips. Triangles are often used to contrast with the appliqué. Pieced motifs, such as Grandmother's Flower Garden or Dresden Plate, can be applied to a foundation and surrounded with a pieced border. The use of appliqué and pieced work in the same quilt can make an exciting combination.

POINSETTIA

The red fabric used for the flowers of this pattern was originally sprigged with yellow. Over the years the yellow has rotted, leaving small holes. These have all been neatly darned. The backing is homespun linen.

The poinsettia (*Euphorbia pulcherrima*) is a Mexican plant and is named after Dr J.P. Poinsett, who first exhibited the plant in Pennsylvania in 1829.

This is a very fine and elegant quilt. The formality of the repeating design is well counter-balanced by the sweeping crescents of a graceful scalloped border. The diamonds making up the poinsettias are first pieced together, and then appliquéd to the background. The rest of the design is directly applied.

The quilt is thinly padded. The plain blocks are quilted with pineapples, with vertical lines behind them. Vertical lines are also quilted behind some of the appliqué, and down the border scallops. The border is edged with a narrow binding.

SIZE
Approximately 96½in × 84in (245cm × 214.5cm)

MATERIALS REQUIRED
All fabrics 45in (115cm) wide
For main blocks, side and corner triangles and border:
7yds (6.4m) of white cotton
For pieced work and appliqué: 2¼yds (2.1m) of red cotton and the same of green cotton
For the backing: 5½yds (5m) of fine, white cotton
5½yds (5m) of cotton or polyester batting
Matching threads

Marking and cutting

1 Prepare templates (see page 100): scale up shapes A, B and C on graph paper, paste to cardboard and cut out; trace remaining shapes, paste to cardboard and cut out. *Note:* seams are *not* allowed for on templates, so when laying the templates on the fabrics, leave at least ½in (12mm) between shapes, for seam allowances.
2 On white cotton, mark 72 blocks A, 22 triangles B and 4 triangles C. The sides of the blocks and short sides of the triangles must lie on the straight grain of the fabric. Cut out all shapes, cutting ¼in (6mm) beyond the marked lines, for seams.

Made around 1840, in Pennsylvania,
this striking quilt, which has an
unusual scalloped edge, is draped over a
field bed. The wood panelling behind
the bed, with its attractive stencilled
pattern, dates from about 1830.

3 In the same way, mark and cut appliqué and pieced-work shapes. One side of the diamonds (D), and the straight edges of the urns (E and F) must lie on the straight grain of the fabric. The straight grain on the scallops must run across from point to point.

On the *wrong* side of the red cotton, mark and cut out 756 diamonds (D) for piecing the flowers.

On the *right* side of the red fabric, mark and cut out 74 side scallops (H), and 4 inner corner scallops (J).

On the *wrong* side of the green cotton, mark and cut out 252 diamonds (D) for the calyces.

On the *right* side of the green fabric, mark and cut out 42 urn sides (E), 42 urn sides (F), 84 leaves (G), 74 side scallops (H), and 4 outer corner scallops (I). Also mark out the flower stems, all ¼in (6mm) wide. Mark 42, 3¼in (8.3cm) long; 42, 5in (12.7cm) long; and 42, 6½in (16.5cm) long.
4 From white cotton, cut border strips 5¼in (13.5cm) wide: two 75in (190.5cm) long, for the ends, and two 97½in (247.5cm) long, for the sides (seams *are* included).

Prepare and apply the shapes

1 First piece the flowers: join three red diamonds (D) and one green (D) to form half the flower, as shown. Repeat, and then join the two halves. Press seams.
2 Staystitch around the edges of the pieced flowers, urns (E and F), leaves (G) and stems. Clip and notch curves and corners; turn under the allowances, except where they will be covered, and baste (see pages 97–8). Press and store flat, in marked bags.
3 Appliqué a block: baste diagonal lines across the block, from corner to corner, as guidelines for positioning the shapes as shown in the diagram. Tuck the upper raw ends of the stems under the flowers, and the lower ends under the urns. Pin, baste and then blindstitch each shape in place, to secure it.

Cut away the background fabric behind the appliqué, at the back of the block, and finish off (see page 98).
4 Prepare 41 more blocks in the same way.

Piece the top

The plain and the patterned blocks are joined together alternately in diagonal rows in the directions shown.
1 For the first row, start at a top corner with a corner triangle (C), and join to it a patterned block. Add on five plain and five patterned blocks, and a side triangle (B).
2 Make the second row, starting with a side triangle (B) and ending with a corner triangle (C). Join this row to row 1.

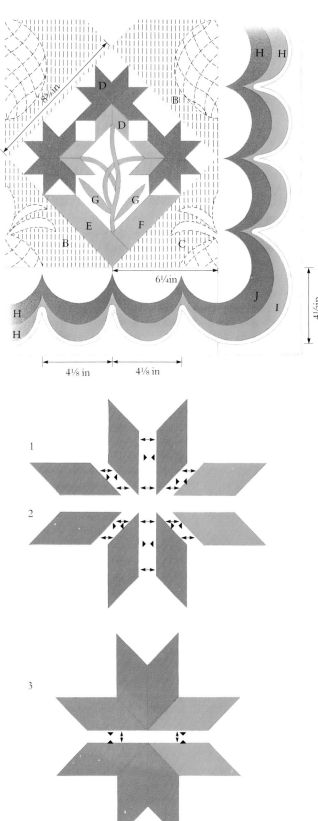

3 Make five progressively shorter rows and join them in turn to row 2.

4 To complete the quilt top, make the other half in the same manner and join the two sections together.

5 With right sides facing, stitch a short border strip to each end of the quilt, and a long one to each side.

The scallop appliqué

Start by applying the scallop at the center of each end and side, adding the corner ones last.

1 Staystitch, turn under and baste around the top edge only of the red scallops, leaving the raw edge around the bottom.

2 Baste these scallops around the quilt border, with their top corners butting against the seam.

3 Staystitch, turn under, and baste around the top edge only of the green scallops.

4 Baste these to overlap the raw edges of the red scallops around the border.

5 Baste the raw edges of the green to the border all around.

Quilting and finishing

1 Mark a pineapple on 30 plain blocks, each facing towards the center, like the poinsettias.

2 Mark ¼in (6mm) vertical lines around the pineapples on the plain blocks, behind the flower heads on the appliquéd blocks, and across the scallops around the border.

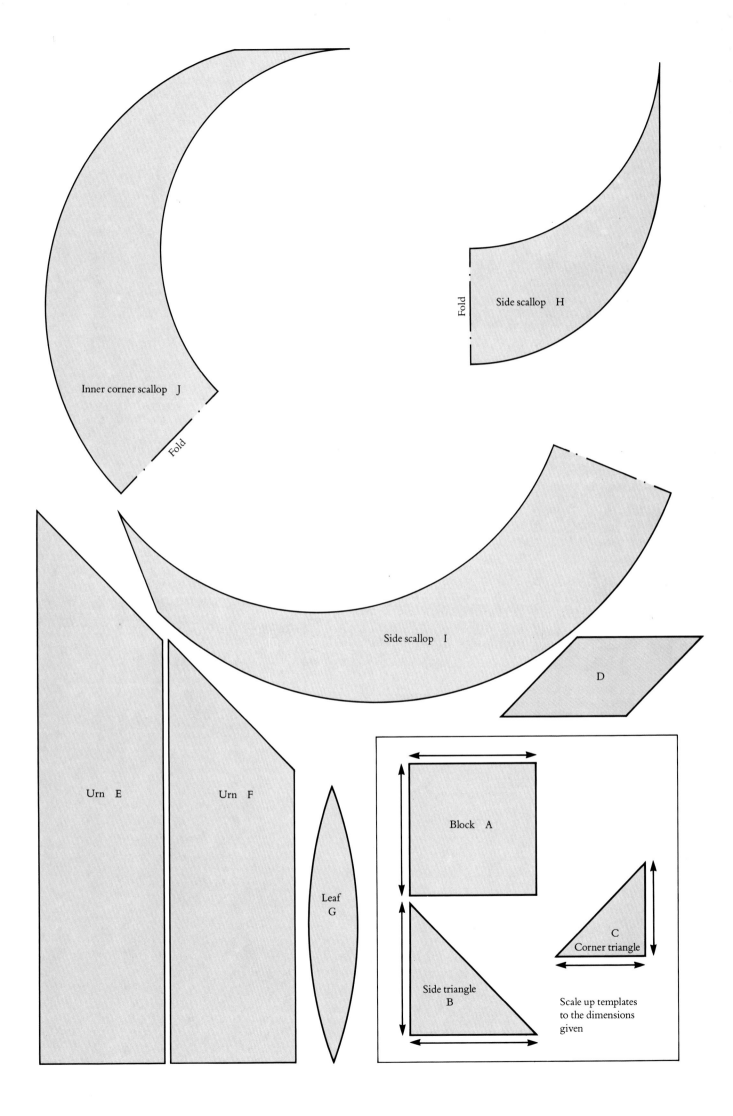

Inner corner scallop   J

Fold

Side scallop   H

Fold

Side scallop   I

D

Urn   E

Urn   F

Leaf
G

Block   A

Side triangle
B

C
Corner triangle

Scale up templates
to the dimensions
given

Quilting pattern for plain blocks

3 Cut out and join both the batting and the backing so that each measures 97½in × 85in (247.5cm × 190.5cm). Extra fabric has been allowed to make the handling of the scallops easier.

4 With wrong sides facing, baste the completed quilt front and the backing together, with the layer of batting sandwiched between (see page 108).

5 Start at the center and quilt all the pineapples and marked lines.

6 With the right sides facing, carefully baste the binding all around the scalloped edge, and ¼in (6mm) inside the edge. Work through all layers of the scallops, border, batting and backing. Stitch all around.

7 Cut away the layers of excess fabrics around all the scallops to leave the ¼in (6mm) seam allowance outside the stitched line.

8 Fold the binding to the back, turn under ¼in (6mm) all around, baste, and hem. Lightly press the edges.

RUTH PORTER'S QUILT

Made of eighteenth-century cottons, this venerable quilt bears the inscription 'R . . . Porter, her bed quilt made in the year 177[7]' on one of the white blocks. This unpadded coverlet has a delightful simplicity, and the softly muted colors, comprising warm dark and light browns, and fresh blues and cream are especially attractive.

The backing and the binding are made of very heavy linen – sadly these are worn and frayed, two centuries of use and laundering have taken their toll.

While the center of the quilt is relatively uncomplicated, the maker had fun with the borders. There are two of them – the outer geometric, the inner a charming array of swags and flowers. The contrasting styles balance perfectly. She did not finish there, but went on to enhance her fine handiwork even further by embroidering an entertaining assortment of motifs, including flowers, birds and even a coffee pot, on some of the plain blocks. Tiny motifs have also been appliquéd onto the little squares of the pieced blocks, and an all-over diamond quilting pattern is worked across the area of pieced and plain blocks.

Probably made in 1777 (the last number of the embroidered date has become indecipherable with age), this is the earliest quilt in the museum's collection, and has a special charm. It is shown against the fireplace of Conkey's Tavern, on which the date 'June ye 21st, 1777 is inscribed.

SIZE
Approximately 99in × 90in (251.5cm × 229cm)

MATERIALS REQUIRED
Fabrics 45in (115cm) wide unless otherwise stated
For blocks and border: 6yds (5.5m) of cream printed cotton
For pieced work and appliqué: 2yds (1.8m) of dark brown printed cotton, and 1yd (90cm) of light brown printed cotton
For appliqué: ½yd (45cm) of blue printed cotton and scraps of other assorted blue cotton prints
For the backing: 8 ½yds (7.75m) either of plain cotton or of a print used for the front, 36in (90cm) wide
Matching threads
Embroidery silks or cottons (optional)

Marking and cutting

1 There are eight templates for pieced work (A-H) and nine for appliqué (I-Q), given overleaf. Prepare both pieced and appliqué templates (see pages 96 and 100), noting that seam allowances are *not* included.

2 Taking the pieced-work templates, mark the shapes on the *wrong* side of the fabric, leaving at least ½in (12mm) between each shape, for seam allowances (marked lines are seamlines).

On cream print, mark 72 shapes A, 71 B, 568 C, and 34 F.

On dark brown print, mark 284 D, 284 E, 172 C, 30 G, and 8 H.

On light brown print, mark 150 C, 30 G, and 8 H.

3 Cut out all marked shapes, adding ¼in (6mm) all around, for seams.

4 Also, on cream print, mark and cut strips for the inner border, all 10½in (26.5cm) wide: two end strips, 50in (127cm) long, and two side strips, 79in (200cm) long.

5 Appliqué shapes can either be marked, cut and stored now, or later, when the piecing is finished. For the appliqué, always mark on the *right* side of the fabric, again leaving ½in (12mm) between shapes, for seam allowances.

On blue cotton, mark 8 swags I and 8 J.

On blue print scraps, mark 4 each of F, L, N and Q, 2 M, 46 O and 24 P. Repeat, marking the same number of shapes on the assorted brown prints.

6 Add an allowance of ¼in (6mm) all around each shape when cutting out appliqué shapes. Staystitch around the edges; clip and notch curves and corners; turn under the allowances and baste (see page 97). Press and store flat, in marked bags.

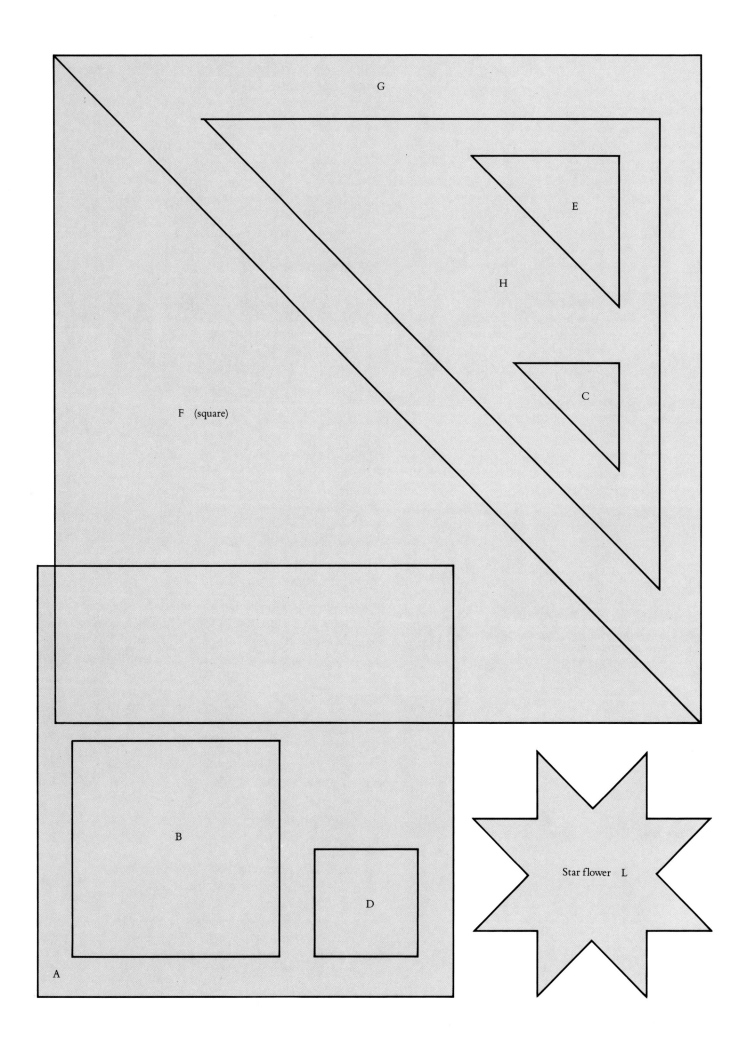

G

E

H

C

F   (square)

B

D

A

Star flower   L

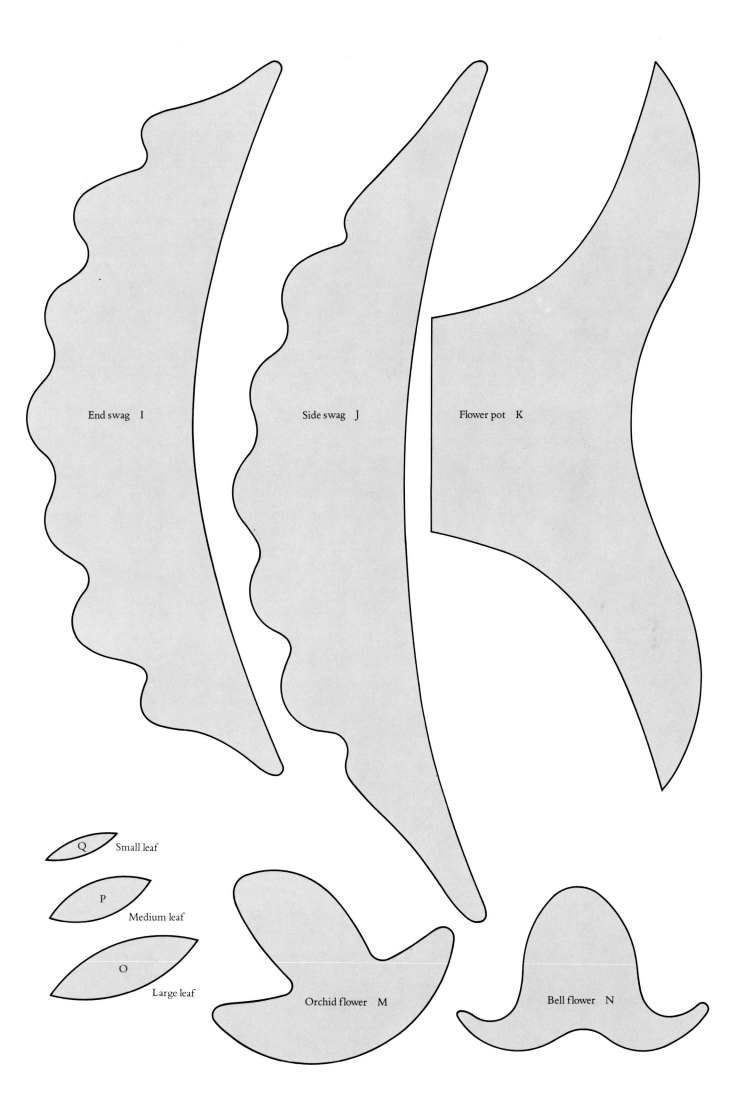

End swag   I

Side swag   J

Flower pot   K

Q   Small leaf

P   Medium leaf

O   Large leaf

Orchid flower   M

Bell flower   N

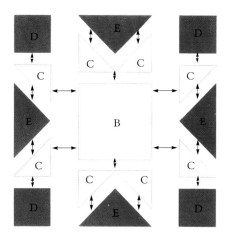

ASSEMBLY DIAGRAM

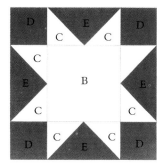

Make up the outer borders

1 With right sides facing, stitch one of the short sides of a dark brown border triangle (G) to one side of a cream border square (F).

2 Stitch a light brown triangle (G) to the opposite side of the square to form a 3-piece diagonal strip.

3 Make up another 25 strips in the same order G–F–G.

4 Make up four diagonal strips in the order H–F–G, and four in the order G–F–H.

5 Join the strips G–F–G, together to make up the two border strips to fit the ends, as shown.

6 Add an H–F–G strip, and a G–F–H strip to each of these four border strips.

7 Add the remaining smaller triangles (H) to the ends, to complete the corner piecing.

8 With right sides facing, stitch the short pieced outer borders to the ends of the quilt, and the long pieced outer borders to the sides.

Appliqué the saw-toothed edging

1 Turn under ¼in (6mm) all around each of the small dark brown and light brown triangles (C) and baste (notch the corners).

2 Baste and blindstitch the light brown triangles around the inside edge of the inner border, with the diagonal close against the seam, as shown.

3 Prepare, baste and stitch the dark brown triangles, also with the diagonal edge close against the seam, around the outer edge of the inner border.

Work the appliqué

The appliqué is all added along the inner borders.

1 Mark the center of each end and each side, and baste and stitch four blue flower pots into position, as shown.

2 Baste and stitch a brown flower pot across each corner.

3 Baste and stitch the swags in pairs, mid-way between the flower pots on the sides and ends.

4 Add the stems to the pots, gently curving them to look natural, and then the flowers and leaves.

5 Baste and stitch three leaves to each end of each pair of swags as shown.

6 Remove all the basting threads and finish as usual.

Quilting and finishing

1 Mark diagonal quilting lines, 1in (2.5cm) apart, in both directions, to form diamonds across the area of pieced and plain blocks. The borders are not quilted.

2 Cut out and join the backing to make an area 99in x 90in (251.5cm × 229cm). With wrong sides facing, baste the completed quilt front and the backing

Piece the top

1 With right sides together, piece a block. Begin making strip 1, joining a cream C to a dark brown D, then follow the diagram until you have joined three strips into a finished block, as shown.

2 Make another 70 blocks to match. Press all seams.

3 Join seven plain and six pieced blocks alternately into a row. Make five more rows the same.

4 Join seven pieced and six plain blocks alternately into a row and make four more rows the same.

5 Join strips alternately to make the quilt top. Press all seams.

6 With right sides facing, stitch a short inner border strip to each end of the completed top, then stitch a longer strip to each side. Press seams.

together. Round the corners slightly, for easier binding.

3 Start quilting at the center of the coverlet and follow the marked lines.

4 If desired, you could decorate the coverlet further by embroidering, or applying, motifs of your own design on the cream pieced squares.

5 From the cream printed cotton, cut strips 1in (2.5cm)

wide and join them together to fit around the coverlet; the finished length should be approximately 10½yds (9.6m).

6 With right sides facing, baste and stitch the binding to the edge of the front of the quilt, easing it around the corners. Fold the binding over to the back. Turn under ¼in (6mm) all around, and hem down neatly.

Bottom right corner of quilt

ORANGE BASKETS

The pieced baskets on this quilt have been arranged so that, whichever side of the bed they are viewed from, they appear the right way up. Each basket is filled with appliqué fruits or flowers. The pattern made from triangles assembled in this manner dates back at least as far as 3,000 BC.

This fresh and lively quilt is reminiscent of those balmy summer days in the garden. Sixteen baskets are filled with an amazing variety of fruit and flowers – with no two baskets the same. The maker simply cut out the shapes, without patterns, and applied them. Lack of space does not allow for more than a few patterns. These, however, will inspire you to make up your own. Work the finer stems in chain stitch.

The quilt is not padded, and the edges are finished with a narrow binding.

SIZE
Approximately 71¼in (181cm) square

MATERIALS REQUIRED
For plain blocks, pieced work, backing and binding.
7¼yds (6.6m) of plain white cotton, 45in (115cm) wide
For baskets: 1yd (90cm) of orange cotton, 45in (115cm) wide
For the appliqué fruits and flowers: scraps of cerise, yellow and green cotton fabrics
4yds (3.7m) of lightweight polyester batting
Matching threads

Marking and cutting
1 From white cotton, cut nine blocks (A), each 13in (33cm) square; this includes ¼in (6mm) seam allowances.
2 Enlarge shapes B-G on graph paper, paste to cardboard and cut out; work remaining shapes in the same way.
Note: seams are *not* allowed for on templates, so when laying the templates on the fabrics, leave at least ½in (12mm) between shapes, for seam allowances.
3 Marking on the *wrong* side of the fabric, mark pieced-work shapes, as follows.

On white cotton, mark 12 B, 4 C, 16 D, 96 E, 16 F, and 32 G.

On orange cotton, mark 192 E.

Marking on the *right* side of the fabric, also mark 32 basket handles (H) on orange cotton.
4 Cut out all shapes, adding ¼in (6mm) all around, for seam allowances.
5 Choose which basket fillings you are going to use (see overleaf for templates), and where and how often

they are to be repeated. (You might decide to create some of your own, as did the original maker.) Make templates for the appliqué shapes and mark the *right* side of the appropriate fabrics. Cut out shapes, adding ¼in (6mm) seam allowances all around.
6 Staystitch around the edges of the appliqué shapes, *these include the basket handles (H)*. Clip and notch curves and corners; turn under the allowances, except where they will be covered, and baste (see page 97). Press and store flat, in marked bags.
7 From white cotton, cut and join strips 1in (2.5cm) wide, for binding. Make a total length of about 8yds (7.3m).

Piece the top
1 With right sides together, make a pieced block, following the block assembly diagram on page 84 and beginning by stitching an orange triangle (E) to one end of a white rectangle (G). When you have completed the basket, add a white triangle (F) to its base. Add a large triangle (D) to the top of the basket to complete the basic block.
2 Press all seams, and then pin, baste and stitch a

The traditional pieced basket design has been treated in an unusual manner in this nineteenth-century quilt. Instead of a single handle, each basket has been depicted as a two-handled bowl, and the containers have been filled with a variety of fruits and flowers.

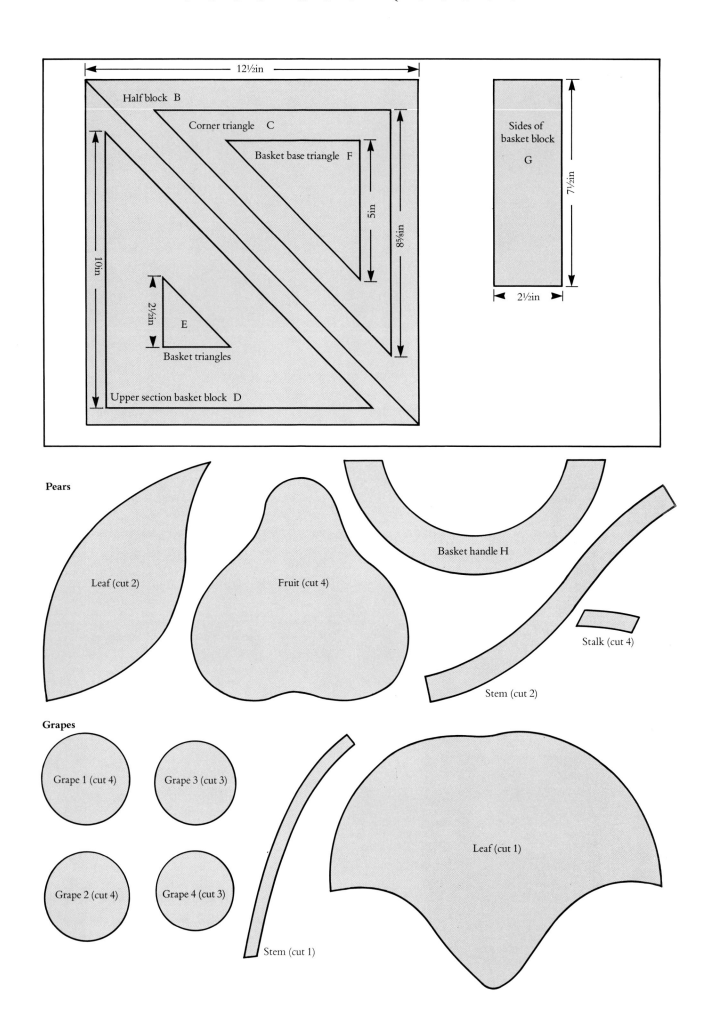

Half block B

Corner triangle   C

Basket base triangle   F

12½in

10in

5in

8⅝in

2½in

E

Basket triangles

Upper section basket block D

Sides of
basket block

G

7½in

2½in

Pears

Leaf (cut 2)

Fruit (cut 4)

Basket handle H

Stalk (cut 4)

Stem (cut 2)

Grapes

Grape 1 (cut 4)

Grape 3 (cut 3)

Grape 2 (cut 4)

Grape 4 (cut 3)

Leaf (cut 1)

Stem (cut 1)

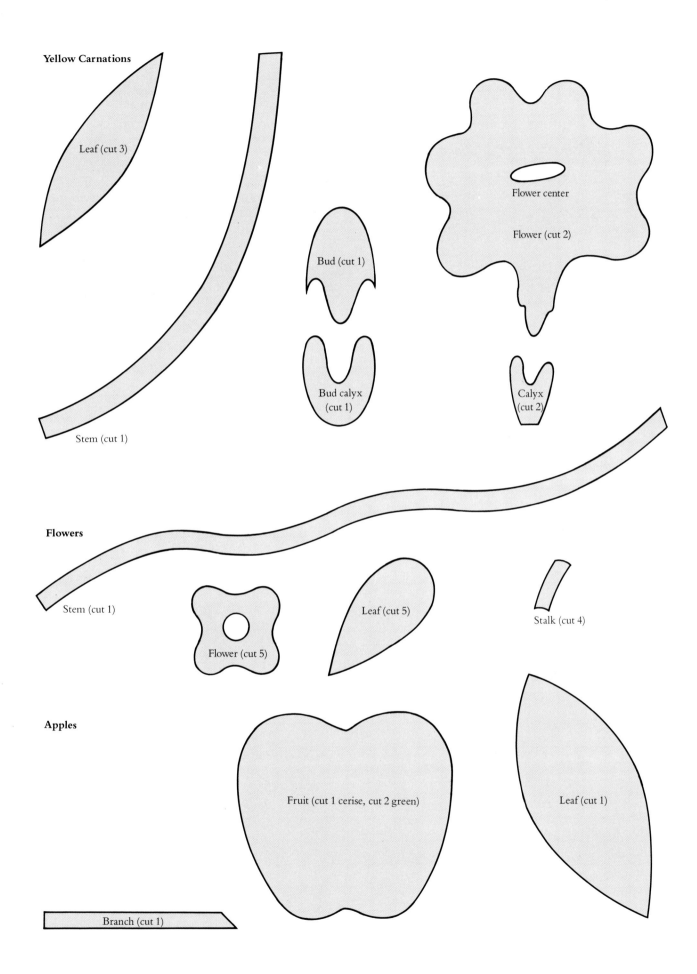

Yellow Carnations

Leaf (cut 3)

Bud (cut 1)

Flower center

Flower (cut 2)

Bud calyx
(cut 1)

Calyx
(cut 2)

Stem (cut 1)

Flowers

Stem (cut 1)

Flower (cut 5)

Leaf (cut 5)

Stalk (cut 4)

Apples

Fruit (cut 1 cerise, cut 2 green)

Leaf (cut 1)

Branch (cut 1)

basket handle (H) to each side of the basket. An appliqué basket filling of fruits or flowers can either be added now, or later, when the quilt face has been pieced together.

3 Complete the remaining 15 pieced baskets.

4 The pieced and plain blocks are joined diagonally into rows: start with a corner triangle (C) and, following the quilt diagram, make the center row of seven blocks ending with a second corner triangle. Make three progressively shorter rows; join them to each other and then to the center strip. Repeat, to complete the other side.

5 If you have not already appliquéd the fruit and flowers, do so at this stage.

Quilting and finishing

1 Mark the quilting patterns (see page 103). Mark a ½in (12mm) diamond pattern on each of the plain blocks (A). Mark the rest of the quilting: double lines ¼in (6mm) apart, with ½in (12mm) between rows, on the basket sides, the basket bases, and the sides and corner triangles. The appliqué fillings are decorated with contour quilting, the lines being set approximately ¼in (6mm) apart, and echoing the shapes of the fruits, flowers and leaves.

2 Cut out and join the backing and batting so that each makes an area of 71¼in (181cm) square. With wrong sides facing, baste the layers together (see page 108). Round off the corners for easier binding.

3 All the basket triangles are outline quilted. Work a line of stitching on each side of every seamline, ⅛in (3mm) out from the line. Stitch the remaining quilting lines as marked.

4 With right sides facing, baste and stitch the binding around the edges on the front of the quilt, taking a ¼in (6mm) seam allowance. Turn the binding over to the back; turn under the ¼in (6mm) allowance and hem down, easing it around the corners.

5 Press lightly.

Side of quilt   – – – – quilting lines

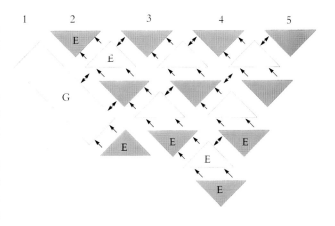

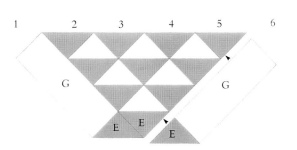

84

The quantities given below list what is required for each basket filled.

Pears
Leaf (cut 2) Fruit (cut 4) Stem (cut 2) Stalk (cut 4)

Yellow Carnations
Stem (cut 1) Leaf (cut 3) Flower center Flower (cut 2) Calyx (cut 2) Bud (cut 1) Bud calyx (cut 1)

Grapes
Leaf (cut 1) Stem (cut 1) Grape 1 (cut 4) Grape 2 (cut 4) Grape 3 (cut 3) Grape 4 (cut 3)

Flowers
Leaf (cut 5) Flower (cut 5) Stalk (cut 4) Stem (cut 1)

Apples
Branch (cut 1) Fruit (cut 1 cerise and 2 green) Leaf (cut 1)

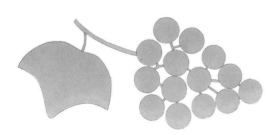

BASKET FILLINGS

TURKEY TRACKS

The strong coloring of the early American fabrics used for the top of this quilt is unusual. Originally, this pattern and its variations was called Wandering Foot, and it was said that whoever slept under it would always have the wanderlust. For this reason, no bride would ever have a Wandering Foot quilt in her hope chest. Because of its unhappy associations, the name was changed to Turkey Tracks, which seemed to break the spell, as it has now become a very popular pattern.

Full of character and vigor, this lovely quilt would be happy in any bedroom setting, antique or modern. The combination of such fresh coloring with a simple, repeating design is certainly eye-catching, and geometric shapes balance beautifully with sweeping curves. This is a straightforward quilt to reproduce.

Elaborate quilting is worked in a charming design of trailing sprays of leaves flowing through all the plain blocks. The appliquéd blocks are quilted in an all-over diamond pattern, and the borders in double diagonal rows of stitching. The quilt is not padded. The self-bound edges are quick to work and make a neat trim.

Made in Maryland between 1840 and 1850, this quilt, seen in a corner of Conkey's Tavern, has a particularly attractive border of delicate bows and swags, thoughtfully cut from a striped and checked fabric.

SIZE
Approximately 94½in × 77½in (240.5cm × 197.5cm)

MATERIALS REQUIRED
All fabrics 45in (115cm) wide
For the top, borders and backing: 9yds (8.25m) of medium-weight white cotton
For the appliqué: 1¾yds (1.6m) of blue striped or checked cotton, and 1yd (90cm) of blue floral printed cotton
5¼yds (4.8m) of lightweight polyester batting
Matching threads

Cut out the quilt top
Note: seams of ¼in (6mm) *are* allowed for.
1 From the white cotton cut 63 blocks, each 9in (23cm) square, with the sides lying on the straight grain of the fabric.
2 Cut out the borders, all 9¼in (23.5m) wide: two strips, 60in (152.5cm) long, for the ends, and two strips, 94½in (239.5cm), long for the sides.

Mark and cut the appliqué shapes
1 Trace template patterns B and C (see overleaf), and mark each with its appropriate identification. Template A is a 4in (10cm) square. (Template C is made in the same way as templates D and H on page 22.) Prepare and cut templates (see page 96).
Note: seam allowances are *not* included.
– – – – quilting lines

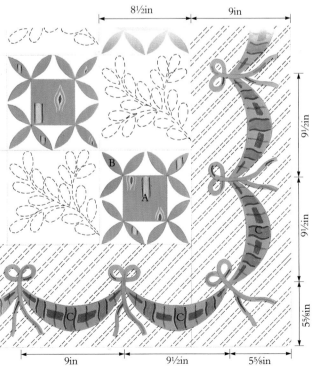

2 As far as possible, mark shapes so that when they are applied their grainlines will run with those of the background fabric. Lay the templates on the fabrics and mark around them, leaving at least ½in (12mm) between shapes, for seam allowances.

On the blue printed cotton mark out 32 center squares (A), with the sides on the straight grain, and 96 turkey tracks (B), with the straight grain of the fabric running from point to point.

On the blue striped cotton, with the stripes and the straight of the grain of the fabric running downwards, mark out 32 swags (C).

3 Cut out all pieces ¼in (6mm) from the marked line to allow for seams.

4 From the blue striped cotton cut 32 strips, each ⅞in (22mm) wide and 19½in (49.5cm) long for the bows (seams *are* allowed for).

5 Staystitch round the edges of each shape and clip the notch the curves and corners. Turn under and baste the edges (see page 97), and then press and store flat until required.

Work the appliqué

1 Find and mark the center of one block by pressing or basting diagonals from corner to corner, each way.

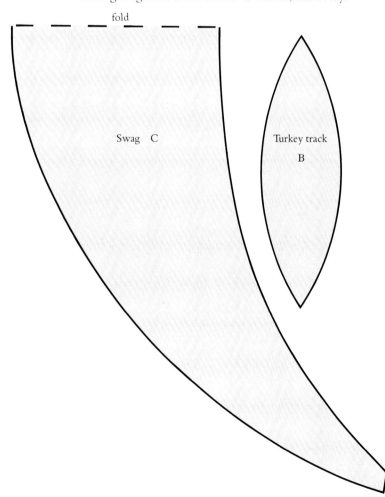

fold

Swag   C

Turkey track
B

2 Baste and blindstitch a prepared center square (A) to the centre.

3 Baste and blindstitch three 'tracks' (B) to each corner of the blue square in the positions shown.

4 Appliqué an additional 31 blocks to match.

Piece the top

Note: ¼in (6mm) seams *are* allowed for.

As shown, the blocks are sewn together in an all-over arrangement of alternating the 32 appliquéd blocks with the remaining 31 plain.

1 With right sides facing, join the blocks to make seven rows of nine blocks. Stitch the rows together to make up the quilt top.

2 With right sides facing, join one of the two shorter strips to each end of the quilt top, and then one of the two longer strips to each side. Press seams.

Work the border appliqué

The swags are spaced at 9½in (24cm) centers along the ends, and 9¼in (23.5cm) centers along the sides. Pin and baste swags and bows into position, shaping the bows as shown in the diagram, and blindstitch down.

Quilting and finishing

1 On the right side of the quilt front, mark all the quilting pattern lines. The plain blocks are quilted in the trailing branches-of-leaves patterns. The appliquéd blocks are worked in an all-over diamond pattern. The borders are quilted in pairs of diagonal lines, set ¼in (6mm) apart, with ¾in (18mm) between each pair. The quilting is worked only up to the swags and bows – not across them.

2 Cut and join strips of backing and batting, making the latter the same size as the quilt top and the former ½in (12mm) larger all around, for the self-binding.

3 Baste all three layers together (see page 108), leaving the excess around the backing free. Round off the corners slightly to make binding easier.

4 Using matching threads wherever possible, quilt the marked lines. Start from the center and work out toward the sides and corners.

5 When quilting is finished, remove basting threads.

6 Trim and straighten the edges, and baste the edge of the front to the backing to secure it.

7 Fold under ¼in (6mm) all around the edge of the backing, and press along the fold.

8 Bring the pressed seam over ¼in (6mm) to the front, and baste down. Blindstitch neatly all around to finish the quilt.

Have the leaf spray quilting design photographed up to fit into a 8½in (21cm) square.

FANNY'S FAN

The arrangement of glowing silk fans creates a fascinating bow-tie effect on this gloriously embroidered throw. Being so beautiful, it is hardly a bedroom piece and was more likely intended as a lap-robe for a chilly parlor.

The maker incorporated over forty different silks, satins and brocades into her masterpiece – and then enhanced it even further with almost the same number of different embroidery stitches! With consummate skill, she stitched every conceivable variation of feather, herringbone, lazy-daisy, chain, stem and other stitches to remarkable effect.

The lap-robe is lightly padded with thin cotton flannel and backed and edged with black printed taffeta. There are no specific quilting patterns: the embroidery follows the outlines of the fans and the blocks, and is also worked round the border. Space does not permit the detailing of the embroidery patterns, but there are many excellent books on the subject.

SIZE
Approximately 62¾in (159.5cm) square

MATERIALS REQUIRED
Fabrics, except for scraps used for fans, 36in (90cm) wide
For the fans: a total of 2¼yds (2.1m) of silks, satins and brocades – Rachel Wintersteen used over 40, and careful planning and collecting will be required if you are to match the beauty of her original
For blocks and border: 3¾yds (3.4m) of black satin
For backing and edging: 3¾yds (3.4m) of printed taffeta
3½yds (3.2m) of cotton flannel
Matching sewing threads
Red embroidery yarn – for embroidery around the edges of the blocks and of the throw
Various embroidery silks – to decorate the seams and top edges of the fans, and to stem stitch the fan sticks

Marking and cutting
1 From black satin, cut 25 blocks, each 11¾in (30cm) square.

Also cut border strips, all 3½in (9cm) wide: two 56¾in (144cm) long, for the ends, and two 62¾in (159.5cm).

Seam allowances *are* included.

2 Trace the wedge template given here, paste to cardboard and cut out. Make several copies to avoid excessive wear and tear.

3 Carefully plan an arrangement of the various colors and textures before marking the fan fabrics. One side of

the template, preferably always the same side, should be kept parallel with the selvage of the fabric. This prevents the edges over-stretching and provides some stability to the sides of the wedge of fabric.

Always mark the *wrong* side of the fabric. Leave at least ½in (12mm) between each marked piece to allow for seams. The marked lines will be the actual stitching lines.

Mark out a total of 225 pieces, and cut them out, adding ¼in (6mm) seam allowances all around.
4 Press, and then work out a final acceptable plan of colors and textures for each of the 25 fans.

Keep each set of nine wedges flat, in their order of piecing, in a separate bag until required.

Piece the top
1 For one block: with right sides facing, stitch nine wedges together in the prepared order to form a quarter circle; press all seams to one side (preferably to the same side) as this will help to make the finished work lie flatter.

Carefully turn under, baste and lightly press the turning allowance around the top of the fan, and also around the bottom edge.

Pin and baste the fan to one corner of a black satin block. It should fit neatly, with the raw edges at each

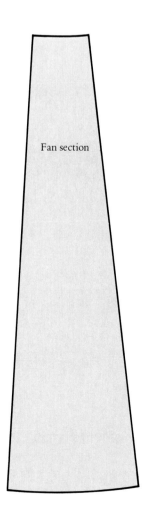

Fan section

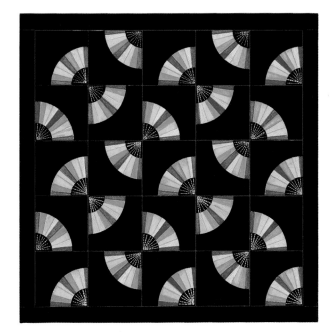

side aligned with the raw edges at the side of the block, and leaving a clear section of black satin, with a radius of 3½in (9cm), in which the sticks of the fan will be embroidered.

Blindstitch the top and bottom edges to the block.

2 Repeat the above stages for the remaining 24 blocks.

3 The next stage is to join the blocks together. Follow the sequence of the 'bow-tie' design shown, and observe the different directions in which the fans face.

With right sides facing, join five blocks together to make a vertical strip. Repeat with four more sets of five blocks.

Join the five strips together to form the 5-block by 5-block front of the throw.

4 With right sides facing, stitch the shorter border strips to opposite ends of the throw. Press the strips outwards. In the same manner, join the two longer strips to the sides.

5 Remove any basting threads and press seams.

Initialled and dated 'R.B.W. 1900' in the bottom right-hand corner, this throw was made by Rachel Boon Wintersteen of Port Carbon, Pennsylvania. Rachel, who was a Quaker, wished to marry a man of a different religion, but this was not allowed. As a consequence, she never married and this coverlet, made for her hope chest, was never used. The bed and furnishings are in the New Orleans style of the later nineteenth century.

Backing and binding

1 Cut out and join the batting, and the taffeta backing, so that each measures 62¾in (159.5cm) square.

2 Baste the completed front face, right side out, to the backing, with the layer of batting sandwiched between (see page 108); straighten and trim the edges, and round off the corners. Baste the edges of the three layers together.

3 From the remainder of the printed backing taffeta, cut and join strips, 1in (2.5cm) wide, making a length of 7yds (6.4m) to reach all around the throw. Press the seams.

4 With right sides facing, baste and stitch the binding around the edges on the front, taking a ¼in (6mm) seam allowance.

Fold the binding to the back, turn under ¼in (6mm) and neatly hem down all around.

The embroidery

The photograph of one of the fans on page 100 gives an indication of the positioning and variety of embroidery stitches in the original. The seams of the fan sections were mainly embroidered in various forms of feather or herringbone stitch – both being wide enough to spread prettily over both sides of the seams.

Red yarn was used throughout to embroider around the perimeters of the blocks, and also around the outer edge of the throw. A diagonal line of feather stitch was worked into each corner.

Some of the embroidery was worked through all three layers, some through the top two and some only on the top layer. There is ample scope for creativity.

A WHOLECLOTH QUILT

BLUE CALAMANCO

No pieced work, no appliqué – just quintessential quilting, with an orderly geometric center panel set in a beautiful sylvan surround. In this, the last in the book, the wheel has turned full circle, back to the earliest quilt in the collection. It is frequently assumed that the first American quilt tops were made of pieced work, but there is no evidence to support this view. The early colonists took quilting skills with them, but there is no mention in contemporary literature of pieced work.

Calamanco, a fine worsted cloth, was sent to America from East Anglia, together with sheep's wool for padding the quilts. Here, several pieces have been joined together and dyed with indigo, but the backing is of natural homespun linen. Calamanco was often glazed by heat and pressure to give a lustrous finish to the cloth. Glazed cotton, which is an excellent fabric for 3-dimensional contours, makes an acceptable modern substitute. Similarly, polyester batting is recommended in place of the original sheep's wool, being easier to quilt and to care for.

SIZE
Approximately 101in × 74in (257cm × 188cm)

MATERIALS REQUIRED
All fabrics 45in (115cm) wide
For the face: 6yds (5.5m) of plain blue glazed cotton chintz
For the backing: 6yds (5.5m) of soft cream cotton
6yds (5.5m) of lightweight polyester batting
Matching blue quilting threads

Marking the patterns

1 Trace the templates for the quilting motifs, A-I (see overleaf); paste to cardboard, and cut out. Make several templates for each, as they will be used repeatedly.
2 Cut the chintz into three strips, each 101½in (258cm) long: a center strip 34½in (88cm) wide and two side strips, each 20½in (52cm) wide.

Made around 1750–75, this fine whole-cloth quilt is shown draped over a folding bed in a room taken from Lee, New Hampshire, and dated around 1730. During this period the principal bed was often in the parlor and offered a chance to the housewife to display her needlework skills.

With right sides facing, join a side strip to each side of the wide center strip. Press well.
3 The quilting patterns are extensive. There are nine different motifs, plus the long trailing stem, and they must all be marked out before the quilt is made up. Following the arrangement shown, draw the patterns around the templates on the front of the quilt.

The background of diagonal quilting around the border runs only up to the leaf, flower and stem motifs, not across them.

Only one side of the trailing stem need be marked. The second is ½in (12mm) from the first and you can easily judge this distance by eye as you work around.

Assemble the quilt

1 Cut out and join strips of batting and backing, so that each measures 101½in × 74½in (258cm × 189cm).
2 With right sides facing outwards, baste the quilt front and backing together, with the layer of batting sandwiched between them. Round off the corners slightly, and notch, to avoid excess bulk in the corners when the edges are turned inside.

Quilting

Use the matching blue thread, and small running stitches, throughout.

Start at the center and work outward toward the sides and corners. Complete the center panel of diamonds, and the two rows surrounding it, before commencing the border quilting.

Stitch two of the three rows of border-stitching, leaving that nearest the edge until later.

Finishing

1 Trim back the batting by ¼in (6mm) all around. Turn the edges of the quilt front and the backing inside, ¼in (6mm), and baste them together.
2 Neatly hem the folded edges together.
3 Lastly, stitch the third row of quilting around the quilt edge.

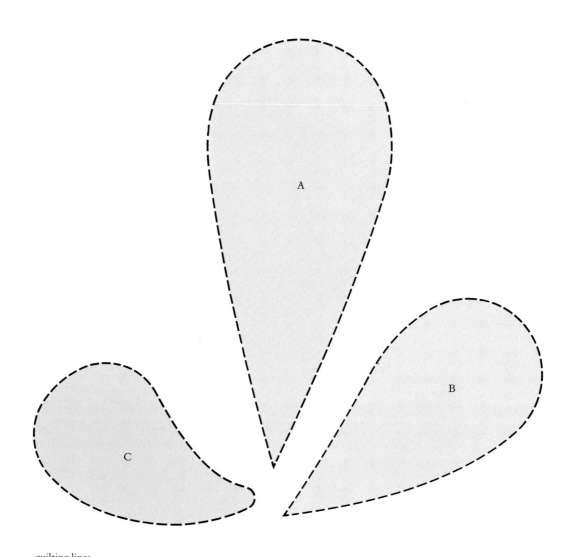

- - - - quilting lines

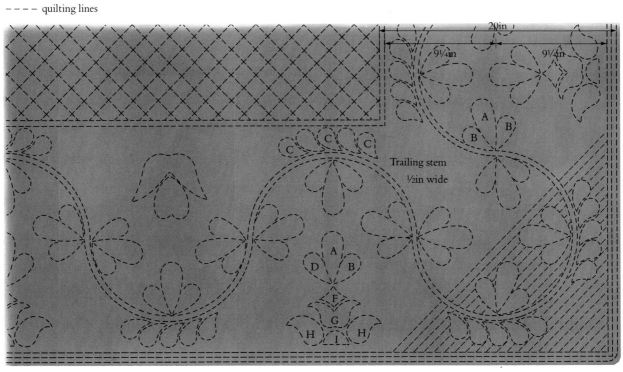

94

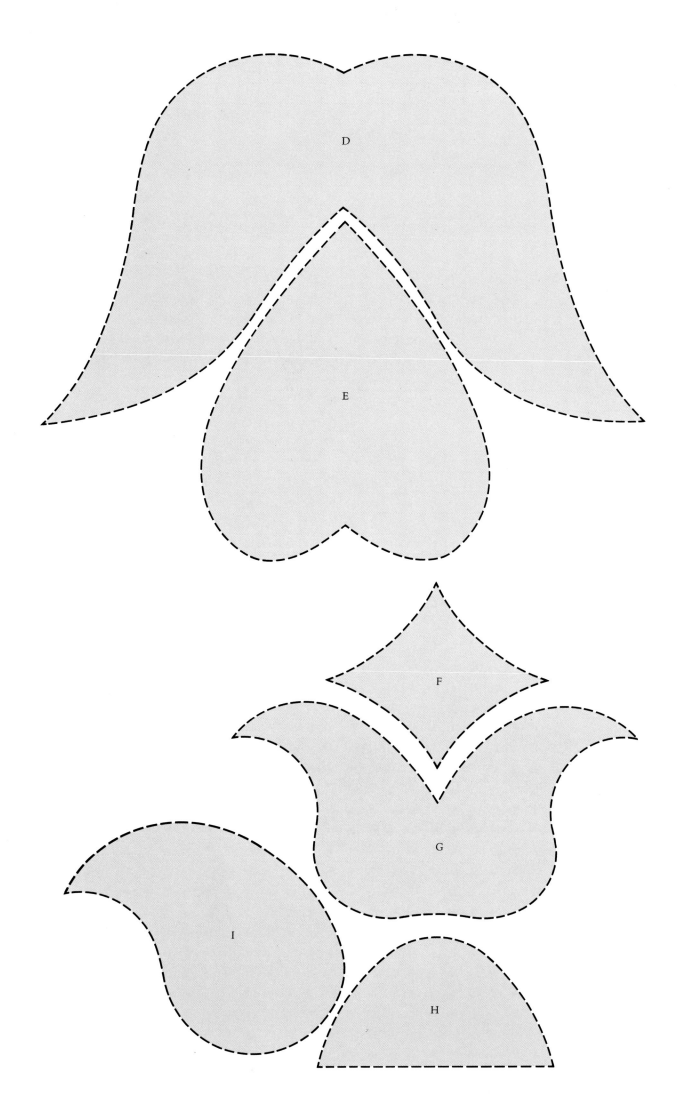

TECHNIQUES FOR PERFECTION

APPLIQUE

Designs for appliqué have varied greatly from the primitive to the most elaborate forms of flora and fauna, geometric shapes, and representational and abstract patterns. In contrast to the angular geometric shapes used for patchwork, patterns for appliqué are freer flowing, with softly-rounded outlines. Many quilts have tops consisting of ready-pieced patchwork applied to a ground fabric, while others may be worked using a combination of patchwork and appliqué.

The naïveté of some of the designs of early American quilt tops is rather reminiscent of the uncomplicated patterns used for tole-work and stencilling, and may well have been inspired by them – or perhaps it was the other way around.

Looking through the appliqué quilts in this book, you will notice the tendency towards using bold rounded shapes with simple outlines. Later you will see the advantage of this when you come to turn under the raw edges for sewing!

Materials required
Fabrics A wide range of fabrics can be used for appliqué, but there is no doubt that pure cotton is far and away the most satisfactory fabric to use for appliqué work on a quilt. It is comfortable and easy to handle, the seams stay put without springing back, and it launders well. The appliqué quilts in this book were made with pure cotton.

It is advisable that the selvages be removed from fabrics before use. Because they are woven to give extra strength, the edges of fabrics have little 'give' and can cause unwanted tension within the work.
For making templates Tracing paper; pencils, rubber and ruler; metal ruler; paper scissors; paper paste; craft knife; cutting board; firm cardboard or see-through plastic. Plastic is easier to use, and because it does not fray at the edges, it is more permanent. It is made in plain or grid-marked sheet, and is available from needlework stores.
For marking fabric A well-sharpened colored crayon to match the fabric as near as possible. A hard-lead pencil makes a good marker for paler fabrics, because it leaves a faint line, which is easily concealed later, and will not smudge.
For cutting shapes Either sharp-pointed cutting-out scissors or a rotary cutter.
For stitching Pins; fine sharp sewing needles; a variety

of threads for basting; pure cotton, or cotton-covered polyester thread for the appliqué. The thread color must always match the applied shape, not the ground fabric. A large appliqué or quilting hoop (see page 109) is a useful optional extra. You will also need a tape measure.
For finishing Pressing iron; small sharp scissors for cutting away the background fabric.

Making the templates for appliqué shapes
Templates are always made exactly to the finished size of the applied shape – seam allowances are added later. Avoid making paper templates; they split, wrinkle and easily get lost or mistakenly discarded.
1 If you are using cardboard, trace the appliqué patterns given; and paste the tracing on to cardboard.
2 Cut out along the marked lines and label shapes with the name of the design, and shape letters and names for easy identification.
3 If you are using see-through plastic for the templates, lay this over the appropriate trace-off patterns given and directly trace each piece. Cut out and name each piece as for cardboard templates.
4 In some areas of the design, one shape will overlap another. Where this happens, the overlap is shown with dotted lines in the patterns. A template for each whole shape must always be made, so that at the basting and sewing stages you will be able to see whether it should under or overlap its neighboring shape.
5 Where there is not the space to provide the entire pattern for a particularly large piece, only half the pattern is provided. Again, a whole template must be made. Trace the half pattern, then, with the center lines exactly aligned, reverse (flop) the tracing to make the other half of the pattern.
6 Cardboard templates can wear around the edges from repeated use, causing your shapes to become slightly smaller, and hence will fail to correspond well to adjoining shapes. It is, therefore, sensible to make several copies of each one, particularly if a large number of identical shapes have to be cut out.
7 After use, store the templates in large marked envelopes for possible future use.

Marking and cutting out the appliqué shapes
1 Press all fabrics for appliqué before marking.
2 Be economical with the fabric; position the shapes

carefully to avoid waste, but remember that seam allowances are *not* included on templates.

3 The fabric must be marked on the right side.

4 The straight grain of the appliqué shape should run in the same direction as the straight grain of the background fabric to which it is to be applied. This will give both fabrics equal 'pull'

5 Remember to reverse (flop) the template for applied shapes where the direction in the design is reversed.

6 Using a pencil or crayon, mark the fabric around the edge of each template in turn, leaving at least ½in (12mm) between pieces, for seam allowances.

7 Cut out each shape ¼in (6mm) larger all around than the finished marked shape, to allow for seam.

8 Store the cut out shapes flat in labelled plastic bags until required for working.

Staystitching the raw edges

Outline each shape with staystitching, just outside the marked line and within the seam allowance (see 1, overleaf). Although not absolutely necessary, staystitchng does make it easier to turn the edges under tidily; it also helps to hold the shape in form, particularly where rounded edges fall on the bias. Use a small running stitch for staystitching.

Clipping the edges

Clip and notch round the curves and corners to help the edges to lie flat and smooth when turned under (see 2, overleaf).

1 On inward facing curves clip the seam allowance at intervals almost to the staystitching.

2 On outward facing curves snip out tiny notches of fabric at intervals from the seam allowance, almost to the staystitching.

3 Clip across outward corners to remove excess bulky fabric.

4 Clip into inner corners.

Turning and basting the edges

1 Turn, press and baste seam allowances back to the wrong side, following the marked line (see 3, overleaf). Use small stitches and work from the right side. Be sure to keep the staystitching within the seam allowance, as it must not be seen from the right side on the finished quilt.

2 It is not always necessary to turn under all edges; leave edges unturned if they will be tucked underneath an overlapping shape. This reduces the bulk and prevents unsightly bumps showing on the appliquéd shape.

3 Should you consider basting all the seam allowances around tiny shapes rather laborious, you can turn them under as you stitch down the appliqué – just push the raw edges underneath with the point of your sewing needle.

Stitching the shape to the background fabric

1 It is of prime importance that the appliqué shapes should lie flat and smooth and their background fabrics – without bubbles or wrinkles. The background fabric should be well pressed before working. Guidelines to assist the correct positioning of the prepared shapes are most helpful. Mark or baste a diagonal line from corner to corner across the block of background fabric. Then arrange the design according to the drawing shown for the individual quilt.

2 First plan an order of sequence for applying the shapes, noting particularly which pieces lap over or under one another.

3 Pin each shape into position on its base fabric, as suggested in the individual instructions for making each quilt. Place the background shapes in position first, and build up the design to the front shapes, tucking raw edges underneath the turned under edges of adjacent shapes, according to the template markings.

4 When you are satisfied with the arrangement, baste the design in place.

5 Start with the knotted end of the thread concealed in the seam allowance.

6 Sew the shape to the base fabric with a small, evenly-spaced 'blind' stitch – a hidden stitch for which the needle is taken through the seam fold of the appliqué shape to the background fabric (see 4, overleaf).

7 Finish off with a knot between the appliqué and the ground fabric.

Finishing the appliqué

1 Remove all pins and basting threads. It is better to remove the base fabric behind completed appliqué, particularly when the work is to be quilted. This is because the appliqué will lie flatter if the extra bulk is removed, and the quilting will later be more evident. Furthermore, the fewer layers of fabric there are, the easier it becomes to quilt the work. Yet another reason for removing base fabric is to eliminate the possibility of a darker fabric showing through a lighter one.

2 With small, sharp scissors carefully cut away – up to ¼in (6mm) from the stitching line – the ground fabric behind each applied shape (see 5, overleaf). In some instances – in 'Rose of Sharon', for example – where there is more than one layer of appliqué, the excess layers of applied fabric at the back should also be

APPLYING THE SHAPES

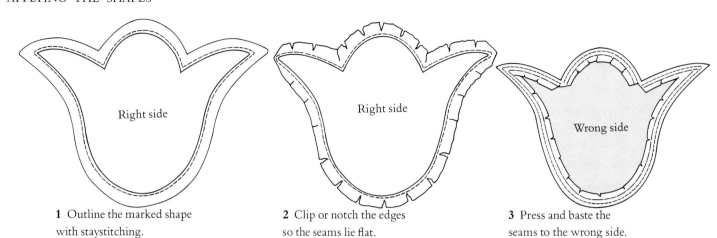

1 Outline the marked shape with staystitching.

2 Clip or notch the edges so the seams lie flat.

3 Press and baste the seams to the wrong side.

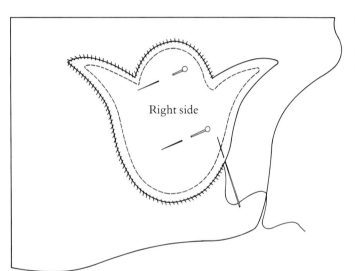

4 Sew the shape to the base fabric with 'blind' stitches.

5 Cut the background fabric away ¼in (6mm) from the stitching line.

Narrow stems Stitch the folded, bias-cut strip to the background fabric. Trim away the excess fabric.

Fold the creased edge over the stitching, sew the folded edge with 'blind' stitches.

Padding appliqué Insert a little stuffing under the shape before completing the stitching.

removed. Cut out the excess from between the rows of stitching on each layer behind the rose.

3 Press the right side of the completed appliqué under a cloth.

Applying narrow stems and thin strips

This is an easy and well-tried solution to the difficulty of trying to cope with seams on long slender stems.

1 Cut the strip of fabric on the bias, fold it in two lengthwise, with wrong sides together, then press.

2 Stitch it to the background fabric, through both raw edges.

3 Cut away the excess fabric along the raw edge, outside the stitching.

4 Fold the creased edge over the stitching – which now becomes one side of the stem – and sew the folded edge to the base with 'blind' stitch to form the other side.

The width of the stem is determined by the distance between the folded edge and the first line of stitches. This can be varied by altering that distance.

Padded appliqué

An extra dimension, for decoration rather than warmth, was given to a few selected areas on several of the quilts in the American Museum – 'Christmas Bride' in this book, for example. A little padding was inserted under the appliqué shape before the stitching to the background fabric was completed. Although slightly raised, the appliqué should feel soft and light. Too much filling would result in an overly heavy bedcover.

Machine-stitched appliqué

Whereas machine-stitched appliqué is stronger and considerably faster than hand-sewn work, it is not necessarily easier. Stitching around numerous curves and angles requires considerable practice, and a great deal of thread. The shapes are applied with satin stitch (closed-up zigzag) and, unlike hand sewing, the stitches are uniform and cannot be hidden. The overall effect is totally different. Never use reverse stitching to start or finish – take the threads to the back of the work to finish off neatly.

1 Prepare the shapes as for hand appliqué, using the same templates. Do not add the seam allowance, as satin stitch is worked on raw edges.

2 Pin and baste the shapes in position on the base fabric as for hand sewing, and stitch around the flat edges with a smooth even satin stitch. Use a medium

A detail from the Pineapples quilt, described on pages 20–24

stitch width; a wide satin stitch looks rather solid and can detract from the beauty of the design.

3 Take the thread ends through to the back and tie.

4 Complete the finishing stages of machine appliqué as for the hand-sewn methods.

Another method of applying shapes by machine creates a less obvious outline than satin stitch, but is heavier looking than a hand-sewn edge. The raw edges are turned under and machine stitched: add the seam allowance to the shapes when cutting out, as for hand sewing; pin and baste each shape into position, and stitch all around, close to the folded edges, with a small running stitch.

PIECED WORK

The angular shapes and geometric patterns used for pieced work contrast greatly with the softly outlined shapes and the pictorial designs so significant of appliquéd work. However, as can be seen in the quilts 'Orange Baskets' and 'Fanny's Fan', the two techniques combine beautifully, and there are other quilts in the book with lovely appliquéd borders.

Pieced designs are based solely on joining almost any size of square, triangular or diamond-shaped fabric cutout to create an entirely new area of material. The 'Stars and Octagons' quilt is a fine example of a totally pieced work quilt.

The methods used are straightforward, and the stitching is of the simplest. More especially, the opportunity of using up fabric scraps and left-overs has made pieced work an economical and popular pastime for generations.

The templates

The template is a rigid pattern which is used to mark out the shapes on the fabric. It can be made of cardboard or, better still, clear plastic which is available from quilting and needlework suppliers. If cardboard is used, it must be very firm, otherwise it will wear down and lose shape. For repeated use, make several copies.

The materials required for making templates are largely the same as those used for appliqué templates (see page 96), though grid-marked, isometric or squared sheets of plastic are particularly useful for the geometric shapes of pieced work.

Templates are cut to the finished size of the patches, without seam allowances. They are scaled up to size on squared or isometric paper, and then pasted to cardboard and cut out, as for appliqué templates. Take great care to cut accurately along the marked lines, keeping the craft knife at right angles to the cardboard – any error will be multiplied across the area of the quilt.

Cutting out the pieces

The shapes for piecing are always marked on the *wrong* side of the fabric: the marked lines can then be seen as the stitching lines.

Remember to reverse (flop) the template when a piece cut from the same fabric has to face the opposite direction.

The sides of squares, and the short sides of triangles should lie on the straight grain of the fabric, as also should the long sides of strips.

Leave ½in (12mm) between each shape, for the seam allowances. Hold the template firmly down on the fabric and draw around it, close against the edge.

A detail from Fanny's Fan, see pages 89–91, showing a few of the numerous embroidery stitches used.

Cut out each piece ¼in (6mm) outside the marked line, for the seam allowances. Store the cut out pieces flat until required.

Joining the pieces together

It is important to plan in advance the order of joining the pieces together. You will find that a sequence of piecing is included with the instructions for the quilts.

1 Place two pieces to be joined with right sides together, and with the marked lines correctly aligned, pin them together. Start the stitching ¼in (6mm) in from the corner at one end, and finish ¼in (6mm) from the corner at the other end. This leaves the seam allowances free for adding on the adjacent pieces.

Stitch along the line, occasionally checking that the marked lines remain aligned.

2 Triangular pieces to be joined in rows should be joined with the upper pieces overlapping the under piece at the top, as shown, to produce a well-aligned seam.

The same method applies to diamond-shaped pieces that are to be joined in rows.

3 Press the seams to one side, generally with a lighter fabric to a darker one, so that the darker color will not show through to the front. Also, the seams are stronger if taken to one side. Do not attempt to stitch across the seams as they will be too thick and difficult to sew through easily. Another reason why they are best left free is to avoid any possibility of tightness at the back of the work.

4 Aim to stitch the pieces together in rows, and then join the rows together to complete a section of the design.

5 Press the work on the wrong side; first the rows, then each block as it is completed. Should you wish to press the front, do it lightly. Use a cloth to avoid marking the fabric, or the ridges of the seams will show through.

Machine piecing

Providing they are identical, pieces can be speedily joined together by machine. This is the 'chain' method, and there is no need to cut the threads between.

1 Pin the pieces together in pairs, with right sides facing, and with the pins at right angles to the edges. The heads should be towards the right when the work is in the machine.

2 Stitch exactly ¼in (6mm) from the edge. Measure this accurately or use the edge of the presser foot as a guide. Conveniently the distance from the needle, this is ¼in (6mm) on some machine. In any case, for the necessary accuracy, the needle must stitch through the marked line throughout. Set the stitch length to medium. Beginning and ending with two or three reverse stitches, stitch together the first pair of pieces. Remove the pins. Do not cut the threads.

3 Bring the next pair along and repeat the processes. Continue the chain until the required number of pairs of pieces have been joined together. Cut and trim the threads between each.

4 Unlike the seams of hand-sewn pieced work, machined seams should be pressed open flat – the machine can cope with the extra thicknesses of fabric. Press seams as you progress, and before adjacent pieces are added.

5 When the required number of blocks have been made and pressed, they are ready for assembly to form the quilt top.

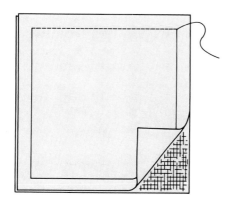

Stitch together the first pair of pieces.

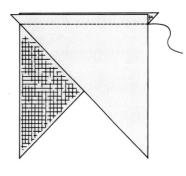

The upper piece overlaps the under piece for a well-aligned seam.

Do not cut the threads. Continue the chain until the required number of pieces are joined.

QUILTING

In this book, the quilting generally reflects the shape and outline of the pieced and appliqué work through which it is stitched, and complements it. However, in one or two of the quilts, the quilting patterns appear to pay little regard to the design over which they are worked. Paradoxically, this in no way detracts from the charm of such quilts – in fact, it can add to it.

Quilting is almost the last stage in making a quilt. The design is marked on the front. The three layers are then basted together, and the marked lines quilted. However elaborate the stitching may appear to be, it is also functional. Its purpose is to anchor the batting between the top and backing layers of the quilt to prevent it from slipping about, either in use or when cleaned. The degree of relief can be varied by the density of the stitching – the closer together it is, the flatter the surface of the work, while areas where there is less stitching will puff up more and show greater contour. The amount of relief is also governed by the thickness (the loft) of the batting.

Pattern and design

It has not always been possible to reproduce, or even determine, all the original quilting patterns, as repeated laundering and subsequent shrinkage have altered the contours. In some instances, the stitching has disappeared altogether. Although there are countless possibilities when it comes to devising new patterns, only those applying to the chosen quilts are described and illustrated in their instructions. Indeed, you may wish to vary the quilting treatment described for individual quilts by lifting a pattern, or patterns, from another quilt. Several further familiar and well-tried traditional designs, which reappear time and time again, are illustrated in this chapter.

The methods of quilting also, have been similarly restricted – chiefly to the wadded (English) and tied methods.

All-over (background) quilting is a sure way of anchoring the padding. Lines of shell (clam), diamond and diagonal stitching are the most favored by the makers of the quilts with which we are concerned. Use a yardstick to mark straight lines across the quilt face, connecting strategic points in the pieced or appliquéd shapes to nsure regularity. A shell pattern is best marked from a template.

Contour quilting follows the outline of the pieced or appliquéd shape, but on the surrounding fabric outside the shape. The stitching is worked in regular, evenly spaced rows. It has the attractive effect of making the shape look higher and more padded than it really is.

Meandered (bunched) quilting is produced by rows of contour quilting, set very close together; such dense stitching produces a much flatter texture.

Outline quilting is worked on the shapes, the object being to accentuate and highlight their features.

Flat quilting is worked through only two layers of fabric: the quilt face and its backing. There is no padding between, hence no raised contours.

In addition to the background filling patterns, there are the flowing designs used for borders; running feather, twist, plait, hammock and rambling roses rank high among the favorites.

Individually quilted motifs – rose and flower forms, stars, feathers, circles and everyday objects – are among the many attractive designs that were, and still are, worked.

Padding

Carded fleece, sheep or lamb's wool, were traditionally used to pad quilts. Kapok (cotton) was also widely used and in many of the quilts the seeds can still be seen or felt. Its silky fibers made cheap fillings, but it is irritating to use and can become lumpy in the work. Such a filling would be quite impractical for today's quilt makers, and there is now a variety of more suitable batting materials available.

Lightweight polyester is very popular. This is a bonded washable batting that will not allow the fibers to creep through the fabric. The lighter, 2oz, weight is the most suitable for hand sewing.

Cotton or wool domette, cotton batting, and cotton and polyester/cotton flannelette are flatter and heavier battings, but check whether or not particular brands of the various types are washable before you purchase.

Silk is light and pleasant to use but expensive.

Careful thought must be given to the choice of the batting. Bonded polyester is sufficiently bouncy to produce a noticeable and attractive relief. To some extent the filling also influences the hang of the quilt. When finished, it should hang down well from the bed – the corners draping downwards, not sticking out as a stiff heavy batting would cause them to do.

Making the quilting templates

Note Details of some of the more traditional quilting patterns used are given in this chapter, but special patterns used in individual quilts are included in their instructions. Use the same materials to make templates as for appliqué templates (see page 96), and the same basic method. When making templates, if possible, also cut out the center vein or middle of a flower. Write the details of the pattern on the template, also its name and reference, so that it can easily be identified.

On templates for repetitive chain or running border designs, mark or notch the edges at the intersections of adjoining shapes. This will ensure that pattern repeats are regularly spaced, and that the elements of the pattern will fit together properly. If it is not possible to deal neatly with the centers of flowers and feather patterns using the cutting tool, they can usually be marked freehand on the fabric as you work. Store all templates in large envelopes until required.

Ready-made plastic templates of a range of quilting patterns are available in many areas. They are perforated for marking the inner areas of the motif, and if you can find an appropriate design it will save a good deal of time.

Transferring the quilting pattern to the fabric
Examination of the quilts selected for this book reveals that some of their makers were less than thorough in the marking of their quilting patterns prior to stitching. Most of the stitching was worked by eye. However, it is recommended that quilting patterns are marked out prior to stitching. This should be done on the right side – the quilt top – prior to basting the two or three layers of the quilt together.

Hold the template firmly down and draw around it, close in against the edge. Remember to reverse (flop) the template when a repeated shape in the design has to face the opposite direction.

There are numerous markers and methods for transferring patterns, but the simplest are best.

Hard lead pencils, well-sharpened, leave fine faint lines on fabrics that are in the light or middle color range; they are easily hidden by the stitching and will not smudge.

Colored pencils can be used on darker fabrics, providing they are of similar color to that of the fabric.

Washable wonder markers are a mid-blue, and show on both dark and light fabrics; the marks can be wiped away with a cloth or cotton swab, moistened with cold water.

Direct tracing on a light-colored fabric is a quick way of transferring the design. There is no need to make a template: hold the fabric right side up over the full-sized pattern, and trace the design.

Running feather

Outline quilting

Wreath of Roses

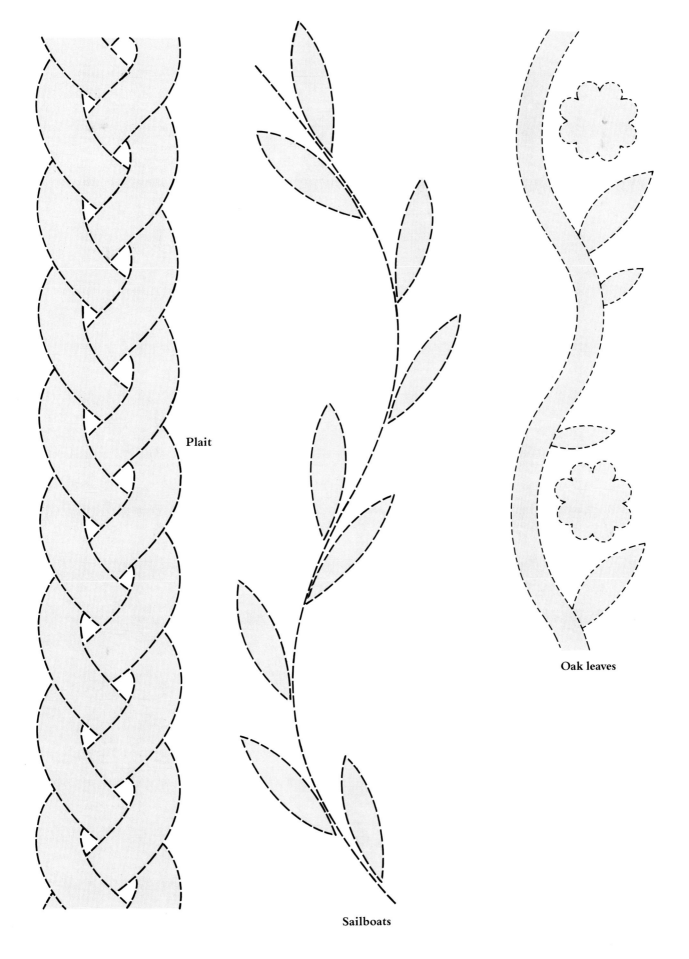

Plait

Sailboats

Oak leaves

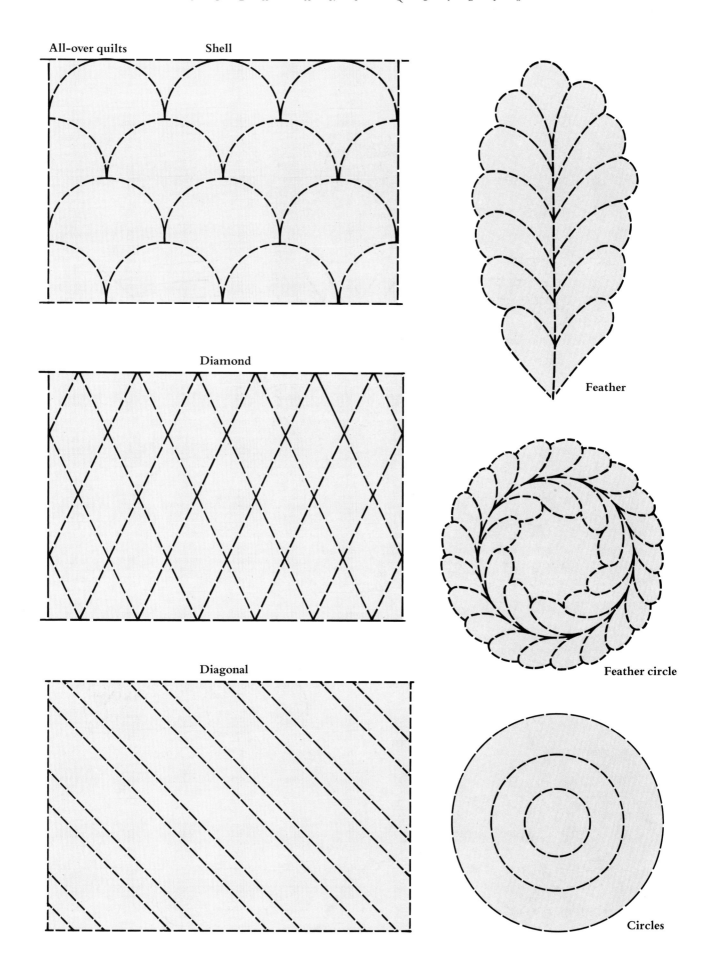

All-over quilts   **Shell**

Diamond

Diagonal

Feather

Feather circle

Circles

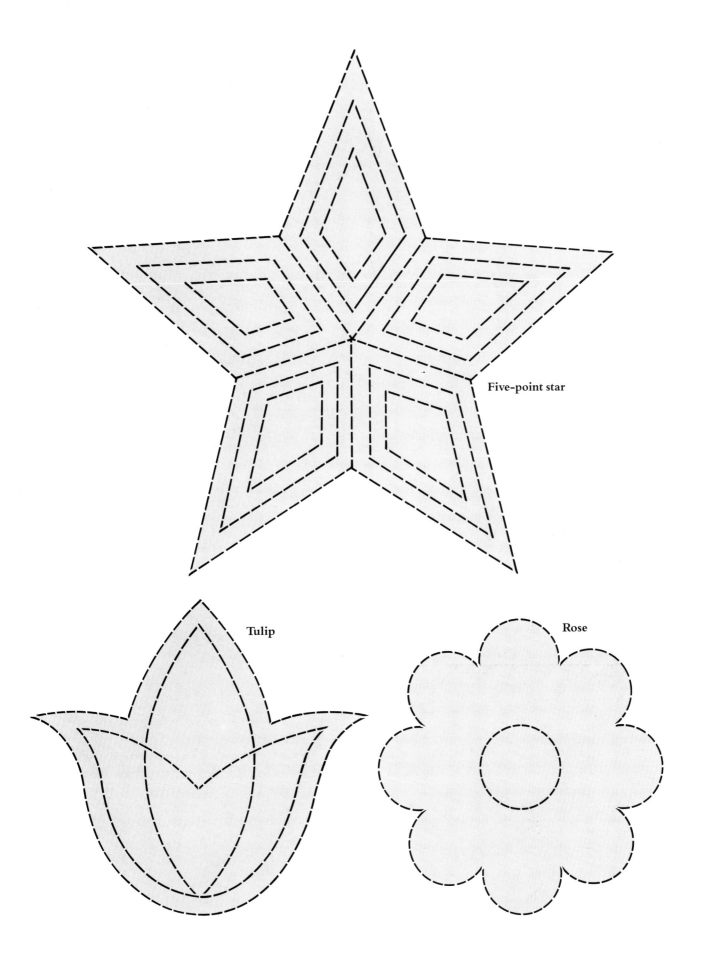

Five-point star

Tulip

Rose

ASSEMBLING THE QUILT

All layers, whether two or three are to be used, must be assembled and basted together before quilting commences. Both the batting and backing should be cut on the straight grain of the fabric.

Lengths of fabrics to be used for the batting and the backing will require joining if the width of the quilt is greater than the width of the fabrics. The seams should run down the length of the quilt; they should be spaced symmetrically, and with the selvages lying parallel to the sides of the quilt. Three lengths will be necessary: the full width of the fabric for the center and equal part-widths at either side to make up the required measurement.

Joining lengths of batting
Lengths of polyester batting should be joined flat, to avoid bulky seams, and with the edges butting together. For this reason, no seam allowances are required. A large herringbone stitch is normally used, though thinner, less bulky batting fabrics may be joined by machine, taking the usual 1/4in (6mm) seam allowances.

Generally, batting materials should not be pressed, particularly the synthetic ones. Pressing, even with a cool iron, can flatten the pile irretrievably, so that no contours arise from the quilting.

Joining lengths of backing materials
Having little bulk, pure cottons, cotton mixtures, and silk fabrics should be joined with the normal flat seam method, machine-stitched for strength and speed. Press the seams open flat after stitching. If you want perfection, overcast or overlock the raw edges; loose threads from raw edges do sometimes show through after use and cleaning.

Pressing and basting
Check over and, if necessary, press all seams on the quilt face, borders and backing. This is your last opportunity to do so for, once quilted, the work must not be ironed.

The next stage is to assemble the layers together and baste. The basis of all good quilting is thorough basting, without which the layers can shift during stitching.

Basting is best done in two stages. Begin by folding the backing, wrong side inward, into four, and marking the center point of each edge with a pin. Lay the fabric on a flat surface (clear floor space, if necessary) and carefully unfold it, wrong side up, smoothing out wrinkles. Tape corners and edges in place.

Similarly, mark the center of each edge of the batting fabric (if used) and then, with the batting folded in half, carefully lay it on one half of the backing, matching center points and corners. Gently unfold the other half, making sure there are no wrinkles, and again tape the edges.

Now baste the backing and batting together. Use long fine needles and relatively fine threads; thick needles and threads can leave unsightly holes and indentations in padded materials. Use up short lengths of threads in colors that contrast with those of the intended quilting threads; in this way, you will avoid confusion between quilting and basting threads when the time comes to remove the latter.

Start each line at the center of the work and move out in radiating lines to the corners and sides, smoothing the backing outward as you baste. Undo tapes as you progress, to avoid too much disturbance of the layers.

There is no need to re-start each line of basting at the center with a new thread and a knot provided that a long end is left at the first stitch of the first line, and not pulled through. Thread the needle on to this end and continue to stitch in the opposite direction. The thread should be pulled gently but firmly, to prevent the layers from shifting.

Never skimp on the basting – work plenty of lines.

Now lay the quilt top right side up over the batting and tape it down round the sides. Smooth all wrinkles outward, then baste through all three layers, again in lines radiating towards the corners and sides.

Finish the edges of the quilt last; this gives you a final opportunity to smooth out any wrinkles that may have collected there.

Pinning method
While the foregoing method is an excellent way of ensuring wrinkle-free quilting, you may feel confident enough to rely on pinning (pin-basting) alone to hold the layers together throughout the quilting. Be sure to buy lots of pins, and watch your fingers!

MATERIALS FOR QUILTING

Materials for Quilting

You will need steel pins, a seam ripper and sharp-pointed embroidery scissors.

Needles Use fine quilting needles, strong enough to pass through the layers of quilt without bending; size 8 'betweens' are suitable. Your needle should be comfortable to handle and easy to manipulate through the layers of materials.

A chenille needle, with a large eye and a sharp point, will be required for 'tie' quilting or tufting.

Threads These must clearly be strong, long-lasting and washable. They must also be color-fast. A special bees-waxed cotton quilting thread is available, but most size 40 to 70 cotton threads can also be used.

A quilting hoop This is optional; while some quilters swear by them, others do not. Round or oval, they come in usefully large sizes, from 18in (45cm) up to 24in (60cm). A word of warning though: do not leave your work in a hoop when you are not stitching. It can leave prominent ring marks and, once quilted, the work cannot again be pressed. When using a hoop, always start the stitching at the center of the hoop, and with the hoop in the center of the quilt. Work outwards in each case.

A quilting frame Traditionally, quilters worked in groups on large and cumbersome floor-standing frames; so large were these that they occupied most of the parlor and had to be hoisted up to the ceiling when not in use. They are too big for the average house today. There are, however, a number of smaller frames available that, if free-standing or supported, will leave both hands free to quilt. Instructions for setting come with the frame, but note that the width given for the frame is actually the width of the webbing, which could be several inches shorter.

Quilting techniques

In order to avoid the risk of puckering, quilting should be worked from the center of the design outwards towards the sides and corners.

The wadded (English) method This is the method most used in this book. Quite simply, the patterns are stitched through all layers of the quilt – the top, the batting and the backing.

1 Use a small, evenly-spaced running stitch, about $\frac{1}{10}$in (2mm) long, that looks the same on both sides. The length can, of course, be varied according to the thickness of the layers of materials; a longer stitch would be stitched on layers of thicker fabrics filled with heavy batting.

2 Pull the stitches firmly to produce the required relief on the work, but not so tightly that the quilt puckers.

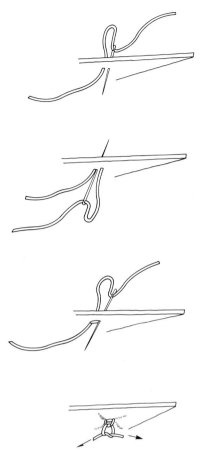

Tied quilting: take the needle through from the back then through from front (top). Take the needle through from the back. Pass needle through from top to back. Tie a square knot.

Tied (tufted) quilting Tying is a time-saving and effective method of holding the layers together, and it can also look very decorative. Use a heavy embroidery or crochet cotton, or knitting wool. Do not 'tie' with synthetic threads – the knot will not hold and it will quickly slip undone. The 'ties' can be worked on the seams, or effectively at strategic positions within the design.

Thread the chenille needle with the yarn. Starting at the back, take the needle through all the layers to the front leaving an end about 3 $\frac{1}{2}$in (9cm) at the back. Bring the needle back up to the back close to the first hole. Take the needle down again to the front through the first hole. Bring it up to the back again through the second hole. Draw the ends together firmly and tie in a square knot: right over left and left over right. Trim the ends to about $\frac{3}{4}$in (2cm) and fluff out.

If the tied knots or tufts are required to show on the front of the quilt, reverse the above procedure.

INDEX

FABRIC QUANTITIES CONVERSION CHART

To use this chart, find the quantity of fabric required for a project, in its width. Look across the chart to see what the quantity will be under the fabric width you want to use. The amounts are rounded up to the nearest ⅛th yard and nearest 10cm.

Fabric width	36in	45in	50in	60in		90cm	112cm	127cm	152.5cm
in yards	1¾	1⅜	1¼	1	**in metres**	1.6	1	1.2	1
	2	1⅝	1½	1¼		1.9	1.5	1.4	1.2
	2¼	1¾	1⅝	1⅜		2.1	1.6	1.5	1.3
	2½	2⅛	1¾	1⅝		2.3	2	1.6	1.5
	2⅞	2¼	2	1¾		2.7	2.1	1.9	1.6
	3⅛	2½	2¼	1⅞		2.9	2.3	2.1	1.8
	3⅜	2¾	2⅜	2		3.2	2.5	2.2	1.9
	3¾	2⅞	2⅝	2¼		3.5	2.7	2.4	2.1
	4¼	3⅛	2¾	2⅜		3.8	2.9	2.5	2.2
	4½	3⅜	3	2⅝		4.2	3.1	2.8	2.4
	4¾	3⅝	3¼	2¾		4.4	3.3	3	2.5
	5	3⅞	3⅜	2⅞		4.6	3.6	3.1	2.7

BIBLIOGRAPHY

Betterton, Sheila *More quilts and coverlets from the American Museum in Britain,* The American Museum, 1988 *Quilts and coverlets from the American Museum in Britain,* The American Museum, 1982

Bishop, R. and Safanda, E. *A gallery of Amish quilts,* Dutton, New York, 1976

Carter, Houck *The Quilt Encyclopedia,* H.N. Abrams, New York, in association with the Museum of American Folk Art, 1991

Colby, Avril *Patchwork,* Batsford, London, 1958 *Quilting,* Batsford, London, 1972

Ferrero, Hedges and Silber *Hearts and hands – the influence of American quilts on women and society,* Quilts Digest Press, San Francisco, 1987

Finley, Ruth *Old patchwork quilts,* Bell, London, 1929

FitzRandolph, Mavis *Traditional quilting,* Batsford, London, 1953

Hulbert, Anne *Machine Quilting and Padded Work,* Batsford, London, 1991

Orlofsky, Myron and Patsy *Quilts in America,* McGraw Hill, New York, 1975

Short, Eirian *Quilting, Technique and Design,* Batsford, London 1974

Webster, Marie D. *Quilts, their story and how to make them,* Practical Patchwork, California, 1991

Walker, Michele *Quiltmaking in patchwork and appliqué,* Ebury Press, 1985.